hyperchoice

hyperchoice

living in an age of diversity

Graham Cheesman

inter-varsity press

INTER-VARSITY PRESS
38 De Montfort Street, Leicester LE1 7GP, England

First published 1997

British Library Cataloguing in Publication Data
A catalogue record for this book is available from the British Library.

ISBN 0–85111–184–X

Set in 10/12pt Garamond

Typeset in Great Britain by Avocet Typeset, Brill, Aylesbury, Bucks

Printed and bound in Great Britain by
The Guernsey Press Co. Ltd., Guernsey, Channel Islands

Inter-Varsity Press is the book-publishing division of the Universities and Colleges Christian Fellowship (formerly the Inter-Varsity Fellowship), a student movement linking Christian Unions in universities and colleges throughout the United Kingdom and the Republic of Ireland, and a member movement of the International Fellowship of Evangelical Students. For information about local and national activities write to UCCF, 38 De Montfort Street, Leicester LE1 7GP.

for my mother and father

contents

preface

What does it mean to serve and follow Christ in a world full of hard choices?

Our generation is faced with more options and with more difficult decisions than any other that has gone before. Despite possessing new tools which help us understand the origins of this diversity and which inform our choices, it is not always easy to know what to believe or which course of action to follow. Faithfulness is occasionally complicated and always thoughtful. This book is a personal attempt to work out a simple, deep commitment to Christ in a complicated world.

I am writing from a position of evangelical openness. For me, this means holding firmly to the historic evangelical faith as expressed in the statements of faith of the World Evangelical Fellowship, the British Evangelical Alliance, the Universities and Colleges Christian Fellowship and especially in the Lausanne Covenant. It also means openness to look at, understand and interact with today's thought. Christians who refuse to do so are not thereby returning to a simple biblical faith, but sticking with the presuppositions of the last generation's thought patterns. Finally, it means an openness to fellow believers. Anyone who professes Christ as Saviour and Lord, holds to the fundamentals of the faith and seeks to live in a way that pleases Christ, has immeasurably more in common with me than anything which could divide us.

The book begins by describing our present diverse society, and goes on to lay some foundations for Christian choices in Christ and the Bible. Chapters on ethics, theology, mission and unity follow, working out just how diversity and Christ in the Word come together in each area. The ground covered is vast, and I do not pretend to wide scholarship or originality. The footnotes are designed not so much to locate the source of each idea as to assist further reading.

My thanks go to all who helped by reading various parts of the manuscript: to Drew Gibson and James McKeown, my colleagues at Belfast Bible College; my friends Norman and Hazel Morrow; William Crawley, whose initial comments were a real encouragement; and Naomi, my daughter, who helped me with some of the history. I would like to record my gratitude also to IVP staff and readers, especially to Stephanie Heald, for all their help and good advice. Special thanks to Maureen King, possibly the best personal secretary in the world. All remaining errors are my responsibility. My two boys put up with a lot less cricket in the driveway and other absences of their father while the book was being written. Above all I would like to record my deep appreciation of my wife Menita, for her advice on the contents of the book, her patience and support while it was being written, and especially her rich companionship over the last twenty-three years.

Graham Cheesman

1. a diverse society

living with diversity

Life today is a series of choices. Melanie's parents chose when she was to be born. Her grandmother took as long choosing between the different romper suits on offer at the local baby shop as she did knitting her first bootees. As Melanie grew up, she began to make choices. There were hundreds of attractive toys in primary-coloured plastic advertised on children's television, and it was agonizingly difficult to decide which to ask for as birthday presents. But she did decide, and slowly she began to learn how to choose for herself. Which was just as well. Soon she was choosing which club to join at school, what subjects to take and which of the many different chocolate bars on the newsagent's counter she would buy with her pocket money.

She decided to go to university, but first Melanie had to choose from thousands of different courses. In her free time, she can choose to go out to one of the many different attractions in town, maybe a multiplex cinema. Or she can stay in, pick up the phone and speak to a friend anywhere in the world. She can settle down with one of the 80,000 books to be published in the UK alone this year, or switch on the television and channel-hop until she finds something among the many programmes that interest her.

Soon Melanie will choose a job (if she is fortunate), a spouse (out of a theoretically wide range of possibilities) and where she will live. Along with these big decisions will arrive a whole bundle of new choices about lifestyle, materialism and what really matters. She will choose holidays from brochures advertising trips to most parts of the world, some of which she may be able to afford.

Eventually Melanie will grow old. By then, it is quite possible that she will be permitted to choose when to die (which, after all, is logical, since her parents chose when she was born). Her family will choose from a catalogue of coffins, and she may well be buried to hymns that she chose herself.

variety

From the first cry to the last sigh, we are creatures of diversity and therefore choice. But this is peculiar to late-twentieth-century western society.

While all human beings make choices, we are a society that has set about creating diversity as never before.

Otube is an older man living in a rural situation in West Africa. He did not choose his wife, since that was the right of his parents. His job is to till the land, as his father did before him. If he wishes to visit someone in another village, he cannot choose to go by plane, train or taxi. He will walk. Emem, his wife, has no local supermarket to visit and no choice about what to have for supper; it will be gari, just like yesterday. Otube's education was the same as everyone else's; he attended the local primary school. He owns the same basic possessions as his neighbours, and he will be buried just as his father was thirty years ago and his friend was last week.

If we exit our culture historically instead of geographically and think back to previous generations in the West, the contrast with our own society is equally startling.

Tesco ergo sum

Diversity of goods, services and choice in general has created a consumer society. Shopping has become a major hobby. Our whole society seems to function on the premise that the 'units' within it are not so much people as consumers to be influenced. We are not left to ourselves to take decisions. Society no longer prescribes, but it certainly pressurizes. There are plenty of groups who seek to manipulate our choices. Advertising seeks to influence our consumer choices by creating a sense of need or a preference for one product over another, often based on unwarranted emotional associations with success or sex. Political spin-doctors or party activists want us to think well of their man or woman. Social pressures from our peer group 'help' us to choose what to wear and how to live, and plenty of people know how to manipulate this to their financial advantage. Choice is big business.

the supermarket of belief

This consumer diversity is one form of pluralism. But pluralism also implies a positive attitude towards such diversity, accepting that it is a good thing. Our society gives people the freedom to choose which set of ethics to hold, which religion to follow, which party to support. 'Pluralism' refers too to a philosophy of relativism, which sees truth and morality not as objective realities which apply to everyone, but rather as different personal values, all equally true.[1] This third use of the word will be discussed in the section entitled 'Postmodernism', later in this chapter, but we turn to the second now.

The Christian sociologist Peter Berger has examined the influence of increasing choice on our society. His initial thesis is that 'modern consciousness entails a movement from fate to choice'. Premodern society had little personal choice built in, and so an individual's life was governed by practical necessity. This necessity was taken as the way things should be – fate. Modern society, by contrast, pluralizes institutions, lifestyles and choices. Again, this is taken as the way things should be; freedom of the individual therefore becomes a keynote in our culture.[2]

The word 'heresy' comes from the Greek word *hairesis*, meaning 'choice'. In premodern society, where truth was seen as one whole concept embracing religion, ethics, politics and all parts of society's life, heretics, who chose something different from the *status quo*, undermined the whole fabric of society. That is why they were not just condemned by the religious, but also put to death by the state. Nowadays, personal freedom of choice is elevated above most other virtues. We are all heretics, and all conspire to maintain that atmosphere of universal heresy in line with Voltaire's maxim, 'I disapprove of what you say, but I will defend to the death your right to say it.'

It does not seem long since we were watching in wonder as the Berlin Wall came down and one by one communist satellites threw off the yoke of the Soviet Union. The driving force behind this dramatic political change was the desire to choose: what to believe, what to buy, who would govern, where to travel and where to live. This is what we expect in today's society. The freedom programme rolls on.

Why are we so keen on freedom? One is almost embarrassed to ask the question, so deeply do we believe that total freedom is a good thing. One reason is that it satisfies the human need for personal identity. Variety helps us to define ourselves over against other people. I am my own man or woman; I did it my way. I am not you, but me. You may go to church and be keen on gardening; I wear jeans and go surfing.

choice and the church

Everyone feels the pressure of decision-making in our present society. To the rest of the world, the Christian church could well appear as a haven of peace because it takes the decisions for its members. Christians simply have to obey its rules. But anyone who has become a Christian knows this not to be the case. Christians are confronted with a high level of diversity within Christianity, and therefore with as many choices as any man or woman in society today – if not more.

Christianity in the West bears a worrying resemblance to its host culture. Christian visitors from the first century would marvel at our supermarkets and endless rows of shops. But they would marvel no less at the vast array of churches and Christian societies, all offering their different wares. They may well wonder whether the consumerism of the supermarket has not entered the body of Christ.

And the diversity is growing. Christians are faced with the pressure of choice in areas never envisaged by their parents. In Christian bookshops and conferences, there is no more popular subject than guidance, because we need help to make the choices.

If Melanie becomes a Christian at university and overcomes the first hurdle by choosing a church, she will not be long in the fellowship before it dawns on her that the choosing is not over. She may well have to take a position on the charismatic movement, declare herself 'Reformed' or not, and decide whether to drink wine, believe in the pre-tribulation rapture or sing modern choruses. Later, having settled down in this fellowship, she will reflect on whether her initial choice of this group of believers was correct in the light of her mature choices about baptism, church government, the gifts of the Spirit and the nature of the Christian life.

There is also an endless choice of charities to support or voluntary societies to join. Christians who wish to serve God beyond the local church can support or join a selection from hundreds of missionary societies or home-based evangelistic and caring groups, from Arab World Ministries to the Zaire Evangelistic Band and just about every letter in between. They are all selling themselves in the Christian marketplace, many looking for Christian custom in a very professional way.

coping with freedom

Diversity, however, is not easy to cope with. Jean-Paul Sartre said modern society was 'condemned to freedom'. We have gone through a fundamental process which has transferred the burden of choice from society as a whole to the individual. We are now discovering just how hard that is. Wide choice is both exhilarating and frightening. The right to choose is heady wine.

Faced with too much choice, we find it difficult to cope. Westerners who spend time in the Third World may suffer a sort of vertigo of variety on returning home. Using a supermarket becomes almost impossible, and it takes time to come to terms with the vast array of consumer choice. On a deeper level, the breakdown of a consensus on values leaves many confused, especially those who enjoyed a more stable, mono-value society in their youth. The West African novelist Chinua Achebe chronicles the impact of westernism on a Nigerian society in his novel *Things Fall Apart* (1958). It would be a good title for western society in the late twentieth century.

Of course, we cannot keep making every little regular decision afresh. That would be too great a burden on any mind. So we programme ourselves to make routine choices automatically; they become habits. Their purpose is to take the stress of decision out of the average day. It is not necessary to decide how to come home from work, whether to buy a paper, which one to buy, or what to do when we get home. Such habits can become so automatic that sometimes we have to ask ourselves if we brushed our teeth that morning, or (worse) kissed our spouse on leaving for work.

mediating structures

For the more important choices of life, we reduce the stress of decision-making by using what Peter Berger calls 'mediating structures'.[3] Society as a whole now provides diversity instead of expectations, so we buy into packages which present us with expectations. Society will no longer shoulder the burden of choice, so we look around for organizations which will do it for us. Young people adopt the uniform of their peers, which may be jeans and a baggy jumper or a sharp suit and a briefcase. Lifestyles are packages of social decisions. Political parties are packages of political decisions. Package holidays relieve us of the decisions about what to see and do abroad.

These structures offer three advantages. First, they remove much of the burden of diversity. We do what the rest do, and believe what the rest believe, within our group. Secondly, these structures enable us to belong. This instinct in the human being seems more powerful than the desire to forge our individual identity. Thirdly, mediating structures lend social confirmation and support to our views and values. No-one likes to stand alone. Lone rangers feel insecure.

Denominations, and to some extent individual churches, are also mediating structures. They are packages of religious decisions, relieving us of some of the 'burden' of our religious freedom. Within each denomination, and across the denominations, other packages are formed, perhaps around popular leaders with a vibrant ministry. Others comprise long-standing traditions or emphases, such as a 'Reformed' view of the Bible and the world. Some packages, such as the charismatic movement, are of more recent origin. Unfortunately, to the extent that we invest our sense of belonging in these packages, we define ourselves over against, and therefore as not belonging to, other packages in the church. And so God's church fragments; diversity engenders more diversity.

packages from the past

One important way in which we manage diversity of choice as Christians is by looking back to frames of reference in the past. At college in the early seventies, for instance, I learnt a great deal from the revival of interest in Puritan writings spearheaded by the Banner of Truth Trust. The advantage of such a strategy is that it takes us out of our own situation. The wisdom of godly people in the past helps us to reach decisions in a more objective way. We are no longer bound within the inadequate assumptions of our present culture. With the help of others, we can judge it from outside. Where this strategy goes wrong, however, is when we allow their decisions to become our own. For instance, it would be wrongheaded to take the Puritans as a package to which we could belong. We cannot live in any other culture than our own. To see the grass as greener elsewhere is a natural reaction to modern society, and many long to live in a more ordered past. Yet nostalgia cannot preach the gospel today or teach us how to live in today's world.

One more point must be made about mediating structures. They no longer command the commitment they used to. Today, individuals pursue their own fulfilment in the midst of diversity, using these structures rather than committing to them. Francis Hsu's influential study on the way we relate to one another in groups as members of western society concluded that the club is the key institution today. We join these mediating structures because they offer us the advantages mentioned above. Should the club cease to fulfil our needs, we move on to another group which more precisely matches our requirements. Thus the very packages which enable us to cope with the proliferation of choice become the victims of personal choice themselves. The nature of our churches, too, is affected by this process.[4]

the creators of choice

What brought about such variety and choice in our present society? Three movements are the heroes and culprits: technology, cultural pluralism and secularism.

technology and diversity

Mainly within developed capitalist nations of the world, a tremendous economic boom occurred in the late 1950s to the early 1970s. World manufacturing output actually quadrupled in that period; total energy consumption trebled in the USA; and unemployment in Europe fell to about 1.5% of the workforce. Technology was the big new social factor.[5]

People in the 1960s were suspicious about the social effects of technology. It became popular to fear for the future of our society: would diversity be squeezed out of the system by the standardization of technology and the power this places into the hands of a few? Jacques Ellul saw humanity as having enjoyed more freedom in the past than in our present age, and had dark forebodings for the future. Herbert Marcuse saw democracy as a confidence trick; freedom is a veneer of unimportant choices, while the real decisions are taken out of our hands. Some of these points are still relevant today. The truth at the end of the twentieth century, however, is more complicated, as Alvin Toffler pointed out in *Future Shock*. Late-twentieth-century technology has increased diversity in at least four areas.[6]

First, technology has broadened the range of consumer goods, while their manufacture has paid wages that enable us to purchase them. Many people have experienced a significant rise in disposable income. Business is delighted, and helps us spend our new-found wealth. Manufacturers of electrical goods present a new type of machine to the public every five years or so. Once we coveted television sets; now we need VCRs and video cameras as well. Mobile phones are now common. Soon, every household will have a personal computer with multimedia. There is often little to choose between different models of each of these products, but the variety of machines to buy and play with is still increasing.

And play we do, because technology has, secondly, increased the amount of leisure time available. Most large newsagents carry fifty or more hobby or leisure magazines offering information and a sense of belonging to woodcarvers, budgie fanciers, hill-walkers, karate practitioners, computer-game addicts, cake-makers, airgun-shooters, radio hams, internet surfers and a whole lot more. Such pursuits are possible because gadgets such as automatic washing machines, dishwashers and microwaves free up the time we used to spend on chores. We can hop in the car and go where we want when we want, easily visiting places in an afternoon that would once have entailed much more time and planning; or save time by doing all the shopping under one roof at the out-of-town supermarket.

Thirdly, the body of human knowledge itself has grown and become more diverse. Speedy communications and a proliferation of journals and publishing houses have been major reasons for this growth. This forces people to specialize if they want to keep up. One can no longer be just a chemist; one has to choose organic, inorganic, pharmaceutical or biological chemistry. One cannot just be a theologian, but must specialize in Old Testament or New Testament studies, historical or philosophical theology, ethics or practical theology. Only then will one understand the journals and feel at home in the subculture of the specialist conference.

Fourthly, and most importantly, technology has prised open the world. The media can bring to our television screens the Formula One Grand Prix as it is happening in Brazil, the lifestyle of a family in Japan and the religion of Saudia Arabia. The global village has become the global living-room. Aeroplanes and satellite technology mean that missionaries do not disappear into darkest Africa any more. We visit them by jumbo jet, talk to them on the telephone and send them faxes or e-mails. We can travel to other cultures and people from other cultures can travel to us. International tourism is easy, and big business. Migration has made most nations multi-ethnic and multicultural.

cultural diversity

This uncovering of the world in all its rich variety has faced us with the most dynamic factor driving diversity of choice today – a fresh way of looking at culture.

The classical use of the word assumes that there is only one culture. It is universal and permanent. People do not possess a culture; they become cultured by the appreciation of Bach, Homer, Dostoevsky and Rembrandt. In Victorian times, this 'civilization' was located in western society. David Livingstone went to the unexplored heart of Africa to spread it among the uncivilized, uncultured peoples of that continent, along with the knowledge of the Lord he loved. Every African should learn to appreciate Beethoven.

This classical usage of the word has now mostly given way to the empirical use: a culture is a set of meanings, values and practices belonging to a specific group of people. We all have our own culture. Therefore, on what grounds can any group claim that its culture is any better than another's, and what justification is there for trying to change other people's beliefs? Because cultural relativism is a significant theme in this book, and lies at the heart of much of the diversity in ethics and doctrine, we shall look at this more recent understanding of culture in a little more depth.

Culture can be defined as 'the more or less integrated system of ideas, feelings and values with their associated patterns of behaviour and products shared by a group of people who organise and regulate what they think, feel and do'. This cultural matrix is not so much taught as imbibed from birth onwards as we grow up in the group, and conditions our lives at every level.[7]

At the superficial level, we encounter people's culture through their products and everyday behaviour. 'Ethnic' shops are popular in the West today, displaying wares and art from the Third World. These products are different in shape and colour from those produced in western factories. They often have a 'basicness' and a life about them which are now missing from most western cultural artifacts. Behaviour patterns, too, differ from culture to culture. Many are associated with food and the use of parts of the body. In some areas of Africa, it is rude to point with the finger, but polite to do so with the lower lip. Because many cultures restrict the use of the left hand to unmentionable but necessary acts, giving or receiving with the left hand causes offence.

Such surface behaviour is produced by a system of values and feelings. Paul Hiebert illustrates this by discussing the way people think of the floor. In western society people dislike sitting or sleeping on the floor. We build ourselves platforms – chairs and beds – so as to avoid the floor whenever possible. We might plead comfort, but this is not necessarily the full story. When a child drops a potato chip on the kitchen floor, he is not allowed to eat it, even though the floor may be cleaner than his hand. We regard floors as dirty. When the chip drops to the floor, it leaves the category of food and enters the category of dirt. We keep our shoes on in the house and church, because, after all, the floor is already dirty. By contrast, traditional Japanese society builds its culture on the premise that floors are clean; therefore shoes are kept off the floor, and sitting and lying on it is fine. This is just one example of how a value or feeling about something integrates whole bundles of behaviour.[8]

Moral values also are set by cultures. James Clavel's novel *Shogun* tells of an English pilot, Blackthorn, who was shipwrecked on the coast of Japan in the sixteenth century and became embroiled in the life of that country at a crucial time in its history. It sold over six million copies, not so much for the excitement of the story as for the way in which, at every turn, it contrasted Japanese and western values. By implication, it criticized our attitudes to honour, cleanliness, death, religion and, above all, sex. At one point, the beautiful Mariko muses on Blackthorn's 'strange' attitude. 'A maid in the night with a man is without import

… pillowing [sex] is a pleasure. Of the body. Nothing has to be said.'[9]

At the core of every culture is a worldview, a belief system about the fundamental matters of existence. It includes an attitude to time, which for some can be circular, repeating itself endlessly, while for others it tends towards an end. It can be regarded as something measured by watches in minutes, or as a series of opportunities to interact with people. This latter attitude is a matter of great frustration for westerners trying to run western institutions in Third World countries.

A worldview will include a belief about the spiritual realm and how it relates to the natural world (and my implication here that these are separate categories betrays my western origins). In the West, when something goes wrong with our car, we take it to the technician we call a mechanic so that he can fix it. When something goes wrong with our body, we take it to the technician called the doctor and ask her to fix it. She might even suggest a spare part these days. Such an attitude appears strange to much of the world. Indeed, it does not work very well. Africans, by and large, have understood that such a model of healing is very useful in certain cases, such as road traffic accidents, but see it as of much less value in cases of chronic backache, stomach discomfort and many other ailments. The spiritual life of the sufferer needs to come into the equation. Western doctors are beginning to agree, but they have time only to be technicians and so they hand out pills instead.

Culture is transmitted by symbol systems. Actions, sounds, money, even smells are sets of symbols. But the most important is language. As we shall see later when discussing the Bible, such a symbol system can be decoded only in relationship to the culture in which it operates. When we say 'red' in English, we mean a colour that is not yellow or green or blue. Or we could mean 'communist', as in the statement, 'He's a red.' Or we could mean 'anger', when we say, 'I saw red.' 'Red' can also mean 'Stop!' and embarrassment, depending on the context in which it is used. It is a multivocal symbol. But it can be decoded easily if we share the culture which defines its use. That task is much more difficult if we do not. Yet it is possible, because symbol systems are meant to transmit truth and feeling to others.

Cultures vary in respect of their internal diversity. Each culture has within it a number of cultural frames which operate in different circumstances or social settings. If an employee dressed and acted in the bank in the same way as in the swimming-pool, he would soon be told that he had got his cultural frames mixed up. Western culture is unique in having so many cultural frames and chosen subcultures or lifestyles. There are overarching cultural agreements, but these seem less significant today than the plurality of cultures which comprise modern western society.

Many books have been written on the problems and opportunities which this rich and fascinating worldwide cultural diversity creates for the cross-cultural missionary. Here, however, we are focusing on the difficulties it creates for the typical western Christian at home. Globalization lands the problem on our doorstep as we encounter the cultures of our neighbours or of those we saw on the television last night. How are we to come to terms with this diversity? The old imperialistic answer to the question, that the traditional western ways and beliefs are right, seems inadequate and conceited. After all, why should our culture be any better than another? Yet if all of them are right, what happens to truth?

secularism and diversity

Premodern societies are relatively stable because there is a mutually beneficial relationship between religion and the *status quo*. A commonly accepted religion stabilizes and unites society, so most societies tend to protect their main religion. In return, the *status quo* is legitimized by claiming that the gods have decreed it. We find this convenient belief in many tribal societies (and also in today's equation of Christianity with 'the American way of life', though that is hardly a premodern society). A stable society creates a stable plausibility structure for its religion. Religions, therefore, do not easily change, and when they do, it is usually in response to change in society.

Because modern society is unstable and changing, religion has suffered. Where only one religion is on offer, it is easy to accept it as true; where there is a variety, how can we know which (if any) is true? A mechanistic view of the world, arising out of the scientific enterprise, has no need of God as a hypothesis. It is perfectly possible to have a secular society which is not pluralistic, and a number of communist regimes have tried to create one – but with little success. Western society has combined secularism with diversity.

Bishop Lesslie Newbigin has described this combination well. Ours is a society where historical and scientific beliefs are regarded as true, but where values and religious beliefs have no universal validity. A schoolchild, asked when the Battle of Hastings was fought, knows that 1066 is right and 1067 is wrong. If the same child is asked whether Muhammad was a prophet of God, or whether sex before marriage is legitimate, there is no right or wrong answer; after all, everyone has a right to his or her own faith and lifestyle. So we become secular in a new way: not forbidding religion, but refusing to allow society to make religious choices for its members. In matters of theology and ethics, we legislate regarding, and disapprove of, only those actions which inhibit the freedom of others to believe and do what they want. In so doing, we hand over to the individual whole new worlds of decision-making.[10]

Such a society both demands tolerance and creates intolerance. We must tolerate all expressions of belief, and all lifestyles and ethical decisions, because we are a free society. But society does not tolerate those who hold an intolerant creed. Thus political correctness becomes repressive, dismissing those who hold 'unacceptable' views about, say, the role of women or the truth or falsehood of Islam. Society has become dogmatic and sometimes silly about its pluralism. 'Proselytism' has become a dirty word; those who want to evangelize, to change the beliefs and practices of others, are striking at the roots of our society because it implies a belief in absolutes: that there are right and wrong beliefs and right and wrong lifestyles.

Shusaku Endo's novel *Silence* (1966) tells the story of Rodríguez, a Jesuit priest secretly landed in Japan at the time of the sixteenth-century persecutions. He is captured and feels the awful silence of God in that situation. His interrogator tells him plainly that he has stepped over too wide a cultural gap in seeking to bring Christ to Japan, and that it will save Japanese Christians great suffering if he denies his Lord. Just as he is about to trample on the image of Christ as a sign of his apostasy, Christ speaks to him: 'Yes, this is what I am here for, trample.' Can there even be situations where it is right to deny Christ for the good of others in another culture? That would be the ultimate relativist act for the Christian.

postmodernism

We must now turn to the philosophical undergirding of our present society which many call postmodernism. Although this is a vague, catch-all term, it strikes at the root of the situation because it suggests dissatisfaction with the modern world as we have known it. Modern society is becoming outmoded. This does not mean that modern attitudes are collapsing, but that we are coming to terms with their limitations. We are losing the confidence which characterized the previous generation.

Not everything about our society is postmodern. Many commentators have fallen into the error of allowing the instrument to dominate the analysis: if someone puts a hammer in your hand, everything starts to look like a nail. Nevertheless, postmodernism does exist.[11]

modern society

A definition of postmodernism needs to begin from an understanding of what was 'modern'. But modern society itself is defined over against what went before.

A premodern society, whether we are thinking of medieval England or of tribal Africa prior to the invasion of western culture, has two important features. First, knowledge is traditional and depends for its authenticity on authority, often that of a religious élite. Secondly, its culture is uniform. Society is a whole entity, with each element (religion, politics, science, commerce and the arts) supporting the others. So, for instance, medieval art usually focused on religious subjects.

The roots of modern culture lay in the Renaissance of the sixteenth century, but its main development came in the Enlightenment of the nineteenth. Its main characteristic is a rejection of traditional sources of knowledge. Authority could no longer decide what was true and right. Instead, the task was handed over to reason. Reason had no boundaries; it had the right to judge all areas of life, whether how a bird flies, how a person should behave, or what God is like.

Reason was the great impartial tool. It led us to objective knowledge and so to freedom from tyranny. The end was the emancipation of humanity, the means autonomous reason. Progress was expected as the tool of reason was put to work. Such self-confidence became linked with aggressive colonialism as we exported this new civilization to the premodern world.

There was great success at first. Modern science developed the technology and communications we have already mentioned. Modern medicine treated more and more diseases, and life expectancy increased. The modern state (another characteristic of modern society) engaged in penal reform and the care of the poor and needy. It did not matter that religious authority no longer acted as a guarantee for the great absolutes of justice, freedom, morals and the like. Reason preserved and justified these ideals in other ways; modernity was based on principles and ideals. Few besides Nietzsche saw the illogicality of rejecting God and keeping morality.

The history of the church in the last few centuries has been dominated by its struggle with the modern mind. The denial of ultimate religious authority led to secularism, as we saw above. The unfettered use of reason led to liberal attitudes to the Bible and questioned fundamental beliefs such as the virgin birth of Christ and his resurrection. The discoveries and theories of science, such as evolution, led to monumental battles.

the failure of the Enlightenment project

The scientific establishment mushroomed in the twentieth century. In 1910 there were about 8,000 German and British physicists and chemists. In 1980, research scientists across the world numbered something like five million.[12] But the love affair with science is largely over today. Science has failed to deliver 'clean' progress. Every advance has cost us something – perhaps too much. Technology and the Industrial Revolution have polluted the environment and destroyed much of the Earth's natural resources. Increased mobility has broken up extended families and the earlier sense of community. Loneliness in the midst of the crowd and stress have increased. Nuclear science, first developed to create 'better' bombs, has come within a hairbreadth of destroying all life on the planet.

The accommodation of the traditional churches to the Enlightenment, and their subsequent weakening (Berger would say 'theological disembowelment'), have led to a rise in unpleasant cults and extreme fundamentalism. Perhaps above all, scientific explanations leave a gaping hole in the psyche because they address the 'how' and have nothing to say about the 'why'. Science was supposed to free us from the enemies that religion could not conquer – hunger, poverty, tyranny and war. It has not done so.

In particular, confidence in progress is on the decline. Any political party that suggested that wages might not keep pace with inflation or that taxes would have to rise would have a slim chance of coming to power. Yet since the oil crisis of the 1970s, expectations of an ever-rising standard of living have been increasingly difficult to fulfil.

Two world wars, the awesome inhumanity of Hitler, Stalin and Pol Pot, and the terrible sufferings in the Third World (partially, at least, caused by the attitudes of the western economies), all cast doubt on the notion that global society is progressing. Closer to home, the jewel in the crown of Enlightenment science, modern medical care, is in crisis. Rather than creating a people less dependent on medical expertise, its growing repertoire of new therapeutic techniques has increased its penetration into the lives of individuals and society. We are all patients now. A medical consultant recently defined a healthy person as someone who had not been adequately investigated. And once the doctors have defined what is wrong with us, the medical establishment can now no longer afford to offer us all its expensive treatments. Modern medical science is, in general, a great blessing, but it has its limitations.

the death of the impartial observer

There is a growing realization among theorists of science that its very foundation – the impartial observer, using the correct method in a rational way – never existed. This figure was, like Superman, simply a modern myth. The biologist and chemist Michael Polanyi, in the introduction to his book *Personal Knowledge* (1958), described his own approach to scientific investigation: 'I start by rejecting the ideal of scientific detachment ... I have shown that into every act of knowing there enters a passionate contribution of the person knowing what is being known, and that this coefficient is no mere imperfection but a vital component of this knowledge.'[13]

Thomas Kuhn, in his book *The Structure of Scientific Revolutions* (1962), questioned the idea that science advances in a straight line as each new bit of knowledge leads on to the next. Rather, it jumps from one whole, interrelated parcel of theories – a way of looking at the world, or paradigm – to another. A few brave scientists strongly sense the inadequacy of the existing paradigm and see reality in a wholly different way. Then a struggle begins between the 'old guard' (the traditionalists) and the new thinkers. More and more scientists move from the old paradigm to the new by an act of conversion. Eventually the new paradigm becomes the established truth, until it in turn is overthrown. This happened when Copernicus questioned the Ptolemaic system, which held that the Sun moved round the Earth, and when Einstein questioned Newtonian physics. Indeed, it is a feature of all scientific progress.[14]

A white coat, or a woolly cardigan and rooms in Oxford, can no longer carry the badge of impartiality. Enlightenment seekers after truth, whether it be in history, science or sociology, are now seen in a more realistic light, as individuals who bring themselves to the task, with all their own presuppositions, inadequacies and preconceptions about what they are going to find. These factors are themselves predetermined by the observers' cultural environment, and determine both the narrowness of their questions and the form of their answers.

the rise of the subjective

Robin Williams, in the film *Dead Poets' Society*, made popular the catchphrase *Carpe diem*, 'Seize the day'. But for whom or for what are we to seize it? In a fragmented world with few if any absolutes of truth and right to fight for, each of us is left with his or her own self. French philosopher Michel Foucault said that self-denial is dead. There is no reason for it. Each of us is the centre of our world. Christians have not escaped this new emphasis on the subjective. Christian historian David Bebbington believes that it lies at the back of the entire charismatic movement. This is too harsh a judgment, but certainly we have seen a shift away from 'What does the Bible say?' to 'What is God telling me?'

If truth is subjective, then it is relative to the culture in which the believer in that truth lives and thinks. There is no reality which is universally valid and can be applied to peoples in all periods of history or different societies across the world. Postmodernism takes the 'uni' out of 'universal'. The great overarching principles by which modern society has lived are no longer seen as universally valid. Reason has to give way to specific reasons in particular situations. What is right and good here and now may not be right, good or useful there and then. We thus generate a diversity of values and answers to the same question, depending on the setting.

bottomless chessboards

Much philosophy now concerns itself with questions of interpretation, or, to give it its technical name, hermeneutics. In modern hermeneutics as applied to literature, we encounter a shift away from the importance of the writer of a text towards that of the reader. As applied to history, there is a shift away from the idea that we can know the past and towards the way historians interpret the past. As applied to philosophy, the shift is away from a concept of absolute truth which is out there to be discovered, and towards our own beliefs or, better, the beliefs of a community. Some postmodern philosophers reject altogether the classic conception of truth. It does not exist. All we have are interpretations. The French philosopher Jacques Derrida has described the situation as a bottomless chessboard.[15]

The contribution of the German philosopher Hans-Georg Gadamer was seminal and deserves careful attention. He too rejects the notion that truth is an objective 'something out there' waiting to be found by the right method. Every interpreter of a situation or a text comes to it with a pre-understanding or tradition, a preliminary idea or anticipation of its meaning, within which he or she encounters the text and engages it in conversation.

This leads to a fusion of two elements, the text and the reader's tradition, making a genuine new creation. This new 'horizon' is in a different place from the horizon of the interpreter. But it is also in a different place from the original horizon of the writer of the text. After all, we can never really discover the originally intended meaning of any writer, because the cultural and historical distance involved is too great for us to cross. So our intention in reading is not to discover the author's intended meaning. We are looking for the emergence of an understanding which is practically relevant to us.

This initial encounter with the text helps us to come back to the text a second time and ask it a new and better set of questions – a process sometimes called the 'hermeneutical circle'. We shall encounter it again later.[16]

Habermas criticizes Gadamer for not being sufficiently suspicious of the reader's or interpreter's tradition. We need to critique the ideologies which create the tradition with which we come to a text, he maintains. We must locate suppressed interests in ourselves and our community, particularly those which are designed to bolster the oppression of people. Clearly this means that Habermas's thinking is very useful in understanding how modern liberation theologians handle the Bible.[17]

Paul Ricoeur, another French philosopher, modifies Gadamer in a number of ways. Perhaps most importantly, he brings to the debate the concept that a text is structured in symbolic form. Symbols are the symptoms of meaning. They need to be analysed and, because of that, we can admit to method in the search for truth.[19]

Today, then, the emphasis in philosophy is on interpretation rather than on 'reality', on the subjective interpreter rather than on objective truth. In chapter 4 we shall see how modern Bible interpretation is struggling to come to terms with this new approach, and how modern theology is reflecting the concerns of Gadamer, Habermas and Ricoeur.

the death of the absolute

The present mood is suspicious of absolutes. Sigmund Freud generated suspicion of our motives by exploring the subconscious. Karl Marx voiced suspicion of the absolutes of modern society by showing how they kept the powerful in power and the powerless quiet. Anthropology attacked cultural imperialism because it was not sufficiently self-critical, falsely believing that the 'civilization' it was spreading was potentially universal rather than just another western culture.

Contemporary politics is a fine showcase for the demise of the absolute.

Protest movements of the 1960s and 1970s are not found in today's universities. Those protests were based on absolutes. The students at the sit-ins or behind the barricades may have criticized the previous generation for holding different absolutes, or for not holding absolutes firmly enough, but it was on the basis of absolutes that they wanted to live their lives. The universals of 'communism and the revolution' or of 'love and peace' were the cause of, and sometimes the excuse for, radical action.

There is a different mood today. Modern students are more concerned with matters that affect them personally as individuals than with issues which their forebears thought affected the world. The great absolutes of this century have produced Belsen and Auschwitz, the Gulag Archipelago, Vietnam and Mao's great social experiment in China. Politics, at least in Europe, has shifted away from theory to practice. In Britain after the Thatcher years, both major parties place more emphasis on good ideas than on ideology.

Arthur Koestler wrote *Darkness at Noon* (1940) out of painful personal experience. In the novel, an old revolutionary, Rubashov, is soon to be purged. In prison, he reflects on how he served the revolution. The historical process was absolute and nothing could get in its way. He lied, send his lover Arlova to her death, and cheated and fought for the party and the revolution without pity. 'The only moral criterion we recognise is social utility.'[20] Even at the end, when Rubashov begins to have his doubts about the result – Stalinism – he still goes through with the show trial and his own execution because he believes that that is the best way to serve the cause.

We move into a different atmosphere in the writings of John Le Carré. He is constantly questioning the importance of absolutes. In *The Russia House* (1989), Barley, the drop-out who never wanted to be a spy in the first place, finally betrays his country. He does so for the sake of one little Russian family that he has come to love. Political absolutes are discredited.

Ethical and religious absolutes are treated with equal suspicion nowadays. Who is right about sex and marriage? The Victorian matron? The sixteenth-century Japanese of Clavel's novel? The young person in the swinging sixties? Or the nineteenth-century African polygamist? It seems presumptuous to choose any one culture and declare it right for everyone in all times. Therefore, there is no 'givenness' about right and wrong. Heterosexuality, sex restricted to marriage – all such were propped up by authority for the sake of absolutes in which we no longer believe. Anyone who doubts the new mood had only to read the agony columns: the basis of advice is never the rightness or wrongness of any action, but what is most likely to make the questioner happy.

Religion too has been shorn of its absolutes by cultural relativism. It is now seen as an aspect of culture and a product of a specific situation. British radical theologian John Hick explains the variety of religions as arising out of experiences of the one God in different cultural settings; we cannot regard any one of them as universally true. In reply to the observation that different religions actually have competing truth claims (for instance, Christianity says that Christ is God, while Islam says he is not), Hick maintains that the difference is not a real clash, since we are not talking about truth in the old-fashioned sense of universally true propositions.[21]

In this atmosphere, the Christian would like to appeal to the Bible. But, Hick would point out, Christians have come to different conclusions about the Bible depending on how they perceive and interpret it from their own cultural position. The 'plain meaning of Scripture' may be plain to one person, because he is reading it with his own cultural spectacles. Another person, reading it from a different culture and tradition, may see very different things there, and just as plainly.

conclusions

We have completed our tentative analysis of our society's diversity and its attitudes to choice. How should we as Christians react to these ideas and movements? How do we please God by our choices within such abundant and widely accepted diversity? I suspect that Christians have a tendency to see this situation as anti-Christian, a case of fight or die. Yet some of the views of postmodern thinkers are closer to the Christian position than those of modern Enlightenment thought. Rejection is comparatively simple. Discernment is harder.

The following conclusions are offered for consideration.

1. *Variety and diversity should be welcomed.* Authority's imposition of uniformity for the sake of social control denies the individual and is unnecessary for the stability of the group. Yet it takes place all over the world. Islamic and communist dictatorships impose uniformity of belief and practice as a means of uniting countries; Constantine found Christianity useful in uniting the Roman Empire. Cult leaders require complete obedience in things small and great, and so turn their adherents into clones of themselves. Traditional Christian leaders, whether the

Roman Catholic hierarchy or the eldership of an evangelical local church, often insist on too much uniformity.

Diversity is God-made. The Christian is free within limits (which we shall discuss later). Diversity enriches. Paul affirms that it is only 'together with all the saints' that we shall comprehend the fullness of the love of God (Eph. 3:18). To make all the saints the same is to impoverish our knowledge of God himself.

2. *The death of the Enlightenment (or at least its present chastened appearance) is no bad thing.* We should be glad that people no longer believe in the god of the scientific method or of human reason. We now know there is no such person as the impartial observer gaining certain, objective, universal knowledge by the application of the right method. Scientists are still individual men and women with their own passions and historical and cultural presuppositions. They look at data chosen by themselves, in a way peculiar to themselves, through spectacles of a particular tint.

This realization comes as a relief for all Christians engaged in biblical studies. For a long time, we have been told that liberal theories were 'the assured results of scientific methods' applied to the Bible, and that anyone who questioned them was reactionary. Nowadays, we can set aside such theories as worthy of less respect and as having limited usefulness. Postliberalism is now a respectable category. But the evangelical position must also examine its claim to be an impartial, presuppositionless reading of the Bible.

3. *We must recognize the role of the group and its influence over our choices.* Human life and thought are always located within a specific historical group of people. One function of the group is to provide social confirmation of our values and beliefs about reality. In short, a group has a common 'plausibility structure'. It is a gentle haven within which our ideas of truth and goodness can remain plausible. It erects a support structure which helps us to maintain our beliefs in the face of a different world. Our group's plausibility structure is composed of all the aspects of the world we take for granted. It contains all the 'of course' statements we make, everything which is 'obviously' true or right. We do not notice these things until we come into contact with a different culture, or until our culture shifts and a different plausibility structure is created.

In October 1553, John Calvin, having accused Michael Servetus of heresy before the magistrates of Geneva, consented to his death. Servetus was burned for his beliefs about the Trinity. Calvin would have preferred beheading as a less painful end, but he wanted Servetus to die because he was a heretic. This was the common position of the Reformers, indeed of virtually everyone in the sixteenth century.[22] If murderers of the body deserved to die, how much more the murderers of the soul? If Servetus had been left to preach, he might have deceived others, to their eternal loss. These seemed good arguments to people at that time. We, by contrast, condemn Iran's death sentence against Salman Rushdie. Why do we think it wrong to burn heretics? Because the plausibility structure of western society has shifted.

In fact, it has not just shifted; it has broken up. Traditional society, which used to provide a single plausibility structure, has fragmented and so has created a plurality of values. This helps to explain why certain beliefs are obvious to some while opposing beliefs are obvious to others. Each group is operating from different plausibility structures. This insight will be of great use to us later when we come to discuss the unity of the church (chapter 6).

4. *We must reject cultural absolutism.* This sees everything 'good' or 'bad' in one's own culture as universally good or bad for all time. Nothing is relative to the age or changes with the situation; everything is absolute. If what I am doing is good and right here and now, it must be good and right for all people everywhere and at all times. It is this attitude which sent missionaries to build English churches in Ghana, told South Sea Island men to wear shirt and trousers and held the weekly prayer meeting on Tuesday nights, just as at home. It is absolutists who talk of 'the plain meaning of Scripture' when what they mean is Scripture as read through their cultural lenses while sitting comfortably within their own plausibility structure. Sometimes this has repulsive results, as when it provided a religious backing for apartheid in South Africa.

5. *We must equally reject total relativism.* Relativism is the idea that there is no objective truth, no objective right or wrong, no certainty. Such a theory is self-contradictory ('Everything is relative' is an absolute statement) and destroys itself from within. Relativism is itself simply one cultural attempt to make claims about reality. Should it ask to be regarded as a universal truth, it falls by its own hand; if nothing has universal significance, neither has western postmodernism.

Against this, Christians affirm the concept of revelation as a category not sufficiently recognized by relativists. God reveals himself as the universal truth and rightness. We are imperfect, culture-bound interpreters, but God exists and it is to him that we must strive to conform our thoughts and our beliefs about what is right. If he exists and speaks, it is reasonable to assume that he would supervise the means of his communication to us so that it conveys the truth. We can, then, trust the Bible. If

Christ is the only way to God, other religions are not valid ways, and the scandal of proselytization becomes a task of love.

6. *Christianity has a great deal to offer our present society*. Fragmented as it is with its diversity of cultures and conflicting truth claims, our culture has given up on objective truth and the idea of plain right and wrong. It has done so because it has no solid reference point outside itself from which these things can be derived. Christians say that Christ supplies the reference point which brings order to our minds, a guide to our consciences and unity to our lives. It is to this that we turn in the next chapter.

2. the basis for Christian choice

Christ the centre

In this age of diversity, which forces on us the constant need to choose, we need a foundation on which to base our decisions. For the Christian, this is found in Christ as revealed in the Bible.

Christianity is grossly distorted when it is presented as a set of doctrines or rules. It is not a system or frame of reference which we decide to buy into in order to sort out our lives. Nor is it a negative choice – a matter of deciding not to do this or that which others are free to do. Christians are people who have made the positive choice of committing themselves to a *person*. It is as positive as marriage in an age of promiscuity.

The problem with modern-day diversity is not just that so many choices make us uncomfortable, but that we feel adrift on a sea of relativism. The need for a single, central reference point becomes more urgent as life becomes more plural. There is a crying need for a factor which unifies and which gives some firm ground to stand on when we take the many choices forced on us by our society. Some would say that such a central reference point is a psychological necessity. Christians would argue that we are made to have God at the centre of our lives, with his truth and values radiating out into all areas. In particular, Christ is the centre for Christians.

But even for Christians, there have been, in practice, other central points. Some have used a particular set of doctrines, so that being Calvinists or Episcopalians has meant more to them than being Christians. But doctrine cannot provide the centre. Even the key set of beliefs we call the gospel cannot replace Christ. The gospel is the truth about Christ and his significance, and if it is regarded in any other way it has lost its moorings. Some Lutheran scholastics of the seventeenth century have been accused of implying that we are saved by believing the correct doctrine of justification by faith. We are not. We are saved by Christ.

Others, in practice, have set up another historical figure as the test for doctrine or practice. Christ has been interpreted in many ways. Who are we to add our own? Taking down one interpretation of Christ from the Christian shelf seems reasonable, whether it be by John Calvin, John Wesley, C. H. Spurgeon, Martyn Lloyd-Jones or Gerald Coates. But that was the error of the Christians at Corinth, where some followed Paul, others Apollos and others Peter (1 Cor. 3). Even the Holy Spirit and his gifts have become the central point in some Christians' lives. Yet it is the task of the Spirit to make Christ central, not to take that place himself.

Against all this, we affirm the centrality of Christ himself in an age of diversity. What does this mean? This is what we must now explore.

Christ as the Christian's culture

As we saw in chapter 1, one way of describing one's culture is to say that it is where one belongs. It is an allegiance which is usually tied to a location. Yet Christians seem to have two locations. Paul sometimes addresses his letters to the church of God in Christ and in Ephesus, or in Christ and in Corinth. Christians have a new belonging to add to our old belonging – an extra location. We are in 'Ephesus' and also in Christ. This way of looking at Paul's idea of being 'in Christ' is possibly closer to his original intention than other popular notions. Christ has inaugurated a new creation, a new era or aeon. The old creation is replaced by the new creation. We are placed in that new creation by belonging to Christ – being baptized into him – and we live no longer in Adam, but in Christ. Sometimes this is plainly called a new spiritual location. Our 'life is now hidden with Christ in God', we are 'seated ... with [Christ] in the heavenly realms' (Rom. 6:1–4; Col. 3:3; Eph. 2:6).

This new location has its own culture, its own plausibility structure and its own frames of reference. Christians live within these while continuing to live in Ephesus, Corinth, London or Sydney. Unfortunately, this new set of outlooks, beliefs and behaviour does not develop as unconsciously or naturally as our first, which we learnt as children. But we are given the Holy Spirit, who makes our new cultural behaviour 'natural' in one sense. As we 'grow up in Christ', so we progressively adopt the pattern of our new spiritual society.

This second belonging implies a new attitude to the first belonging. At one level, our first belonging is exchanged for our second. The old reality is 'fleshly', 'sinful', the 'old nature' and 'of the world', and as such has to be fought, rejected or put off. When Paul talks about the 'flesh', he means the sinful principle within, not that our bodies are sinful (the error of the Manichees). That would lead to excesses of austerity as the way to holiness. Similarly, the fact that Christians are not 'of the world' does not mean that everything in the world is sinful and to be avoided. Christians are to contribute to society, not opt out of it.

Our first location, the place of our birth and culture, remains a reality for us. Christ, however, requires our new location, in heavenly places with him, to become the overriding reality in which we live. We are 'aliens and strangers' in this world (Heb. 11:13). We belong in the new culture of Christ; we are 'in him'. We must let the new culture judge the old – but here lies a trap. Evaluating our culture means evaluating its history.

history as convenient interpretation

In evaluating past events, even those of only fifty years ago, it is difficult and perhaps impossible to state precisely what happened and why. Historians have conflicting theories about even the most fundamental events of history, and we can access the past only through these theories. In that sense, there is no such thing as history, only the ideas of historians. Historians are as affected as biblical or classical scholars by postmodern scepticism. Is there an objective reality out there that we can discover, or can we deal only with useful interpretation? Historical distance is as hard to cross as cultural distance. Yet this does not allow us the right consciously to manipulate history to serve a personal agenda, whether cynically or 'for the best'.

Christians do not have a good record on historical impartiality. The faithful of earlier ages are often dealt with as though they were Sunday-school prize-winners. Their faults are forgotten; their private lives and loves are sanitized. Above all, we seek to minimize the cultural distance between them and us. An example from the early English Reformation is Thomas Bilney, who took mass from the hands of a Catholic priest just before he went to the stake for his Protestant faith. Around the same time John Frith, another martyr, advised Protestant believers to attend the mass but to put their own interpretation on it. We learn neither of these facts from popular Protestant histories. Why? Because these early English Reformers were located within a transitional period; lines of demarcation between Catholic and Protestant had not yet been drawn. Two mutually suspicious cultures had not yet been created. Once the lines are drawn, however, they begin to control our selection of facts. So we write about our heroes as if they would be good deacons or youth leaders in our church today.

We unconsciously apply this methodology to Christ, creating him in our own image. But this is deeply damaging to faith. Only a whole Christ can critique our own inherited cultural values, just as he did his own in his disputes with the Pharisees and in the Sermon on the Mount.

Christ in our image

One example of the way we manufacture our own image of Christ is the 'white Christ' of the West. Jesus was Semitic, and therefore dark-skinned. But that is not how we have painted him. Black American theologian James Cone comments that 'the "raceless" American Christ has a light skin, wavy brown hair, and sometimes – wonder of wonders – blue eyes. For whites to find him with big lips and kinky hair is as offensive as it was for the Pharisees to find him partying with tax collectors. But whether whites want to hear it or not, Christ is black, baby.'[1]

Cone is not pretending that Christ was a black African. He is simply doing from his own racial perspective what white Europeans have done from theirs: claiming Christ for those of his own colour.

Anton Wessels in his book *Images of Jesus*[2] points out that our pictures of Christ have usually reflected our cultural viewpoint. The early, persecuted church saw him as Shepherd; the Holy Roman Empire as King of the world; and El Greco in the later Middle Ages as a thin, 'spiritual', ascetic figure. Lesslie Newbigin shows that this is as true for word portraits as it is for oils and watercolours. The innumerable 'lives of Jesus' produced by liberal Protestantism, for instance, were mostly self-portraits, telling us more about the writers than about Jesus.[3] But all such images are generated out of personal or societal concerns.

One of the most blatant examples of this practice is seen in our attitude to wealth. One might assume that 'health and wealth' preachers would face an insuperable difficulty in Christ the poor preacher of the highways and byways of Galilee. Not so. I recently read an article which remarked on our Lord's garment, for which the soldiers at the foot of the cross cast lots: it was a single piece, it said, apparently quite unusual, and obviously valuable, rather like the designer clothes of today! At least that writer attempted to reconcile the life of Christ with his own. Many churches today represent Christ with pomp, ceremony, riches, palaces and titles of honour. These features, present in the older established denominations for historical reasons, seem to conflict not just with the cultural accidents of Christ's life, but also with his values.

the humanity of Christ

Nevertheless, there is a valid way of presenting Jesus within our cultural framework.

On 20 May 325, about 220 bishops gathered in the little Greek town of Nicaea for the first ecumenical or worldwide council of the church. In response to a growing heresy, they proclaimed that Christ is both human and divine, and so created the foundation for all subsequent language about Christ.[4] His divinity is directly connected with the content of his revelation of God the Father. Because he is God, he reveals the character and agenda of God to us. His humanity is directly connected with his accessibility. Because he is human, he speaks into our lives. The divinity of Christ means that he is the one supracultural norm for all of us. What he reveals of the Father is the voice of God, and is to be our belief. In particular, his sinlessness and positive righteousness, revealing the holiness of God, is our example in every culture. Christ's humanity involved him in belonging to a particular culture, but it signalled his willingness to be accessible and relevant to every culture on earth.

It is therefore valid to express Christ in terms of our own culture, while still allowing him to stand outside it and judge it. This has to be so, because it is the only way of making him available to us where we are. Chapter 4, on belief, culture and theology, explores how the culture of a situation affects our presentation of Christ. It is enough to note here that to ask how Christ would address the problems and longings of a particular culture can enrich our understanding of him – an understanding which has so often been constructed out of western cultural questions and longings. Often, a new method of scaffolding is required before we can build new, beautiful and valid sections of Christology. To bring Christ to a new culture is to look for a contribution from that culture to the ongoing task of the church in understanding Christ.

Christ as central motive

Why do we believe what we believe and do what we do? With this question we enter the territory of motive, where it is difficult to find our way. Few would deny that Freud's elucidation of the unconscious was broadly correct, even though they may disagree with the way he drew its maps. He showed us that there are always more than surface reasons for our reasons; there are hidden motives in even our desire for the right motives. Each action or belief has many levels of motivation. We have already mentioned the part our society and culture play in shaping us, creating our plausibility structures and our sense of right and wrong. As individuals, our natural bent towards certain attitudes and actions is influenced also by our personality, that is, the interaction of our genes and our experiences.

For instance, when Christians move to a new town to work or study, they often choose a place of worship where they 'feel comfortable' without analysing this feeling too closely. The motive for that choice (indeed any such Christian choice) is probably a complicated bundle of factors. Our choices are not just rational; they are biological and emotional, and influenced by our individual histories.

In the New Testament we can trace an interesting shift of motive. During Christ's ministry on earth, we see him doing everything for the Father, to bring in the kingdom of God. He had this single aim, and taught his disciples also to seek first the kingdom of God. Do this, he said, and all other matters will fall into place. Then came his death and resurrection. He appeared to his disciples and told them that all authority in heaven and on earth had been given to him. They must therefore go into all the world, exhorting everyone everywhere to recognize this new fact and to bow the knee to him, to declare him Lord in the world and in their lives. Thus the risen Christ himself, and his lordship, become the focus. The phrase 'Jesus is Lord' was the first Christian creed. Paul is a good example of a post-resurrection disciple. He once stated that 'to me, to live is Christ' (Phil. 1:21). To know and to live for Christ was his great life motive. It controlled his beliefs, his service and his holiness. If asked why, he would have said, 'Because Christ *is* Lord.' He was merely working out a cosmic reality in his own life, in gratitude for what Christ had done for him.

getting motives right

As Christians we have an ongoing programme of simplifying our motives and getting them in the right order. We wish to place Christ at number one on the list and then reduce the impact on decision-making of numbers two, three and four. We are aiming for singleness of purpose, sometimes called consecration. Even good motives need to be kept in the right order. Love for others, for instance, must always take second place to love for Christ, and arise out of that love.

Some years ago, a Christian girl I knew became pregnant outside marriage. The relationship broke up and she was left alone to bring up the child. Life was difficult. When the child was only a few years old, a fine Christian fellow fell in love with the young woman and eventually they got married. It was a happy ending to a sad situation. The point is this. Her fiancé loved the young woman for herself. At first, he loved her little boy for her sake and in relation to his love for her. That is how the Christian loves the world. As Dietrich Bonhoeffer writes in his book *Life*

Together, Christian fellowship at its best is a mediate rather than an immediate love. Immediate love is not wrong. But any immediate love stronger than the love we have for Christ is idolatry.[5]

Christ as all

Finally, Christ invites us to turn away from ourselves as the central point and motive for our lives and to turn to God. New life in Christ requires a death to ourselves, 'taking up the cross', just as Jesus died to himself. But of all our tasks in life, this reorientation of our motives away from ourselves is the most difficult and painful. In a chapter headed 'On the few lovers of the cross of Jesus', Thomas à Kempis says: 'Jesus has many who love His Kingdom in Heaven, but few who bear his Cross. He has many who desire comfort, but few who desire suffering. He finds many to share His feast, but few His fasting. All desire to rejoice with Him, but few are willing to suffer for His sake ... Those who love Jesus for His own sake and not for the sake of comfort for themselves, bless Him in every trial and anguish of heart, no less than in the greatest joy ... Oh how powerful is the love of Jesus, free from all self-interest and self-love! ... [but] seldom is anyone so spiritual as to strip himself entirely of self-love.'[6]

The converse of this death of self is entry into a new life of relationship with God. Christ died to bring us back to God, to forge again the relationship between sinful men and women and a holy God. To keep that fact central is to keep the relationship central in our lives. In other words, the life of prayer and devotion itself acknowledges the centrality of Christ. This is reinforced by Christ's example while he was on earth. The great writers on prayer from St Bernard to Thomas Merton wrote about something that was not peripheral but central in the Christian life – our transformation into that for which we were redeemed by Christ.

'To me, to live is Christ,' wrote Paul (Phil. 1:21). The rest of the book attempts to explore how this works out in practice.

why christ?

But why Christ amid the diversity of religions today? This is an insistent question for many thinking Christians. It also presents us with difficulty in evangelism. I remember a young man, his head full of materialism and plans to climb the social ladder. When I asked him to consider Christ, he replied that if he did, he would in all honesty have to consider Buddha and Muhammad as well.

The question 'Why Christ rather than Muhammad, Buddha or Confucius?' is a very old one for Christians in Cairo or Tokyo; it comes as a bit of a shock to Christians in Tunbridge Wells. But not as much of a shock as it would have been twenty years ago. We are no longer in a mono-religious culture. Just as the corner shop which sold flour by the pound has given way to the supermarket which markets half a dozen brands in kilos, the Christianity of the West has given way to pluralism in religion.

The communications explosion has brought all the major religions of the world into our home. The migration of peoples, particularly from the Indian subcontinent and Asia, has created significant communities of other faiths within our society. Mosques and Hindu cultural centres are now dotted across most western countries, and many of these faiths are increasingly seeing the host culture as a target for mission. These developments have prompted the rise of a new discipline, comparative religion or the phenomenology of religion, as scholars and theologians interact with this new material. Most importantly, our access to these religions, and their adherents' exposure to our culture, has engendered a pluralistic, relativistic mood. Today, we are inclined to accept all faiths on their own terms as valid life choices alongside Christianity, which has held the field for so long.

religious relativism

The common understanding in this new situation has been that religion is a culturally relative phenomenon. Christianity has been the religion of the West just as Hinduism covers much of India and Islam is for the Arabs. One culture is not necessarily better than another, and the same is true of religion. To claim that one religion has the truth and that all others are in error is regarded as narrow-minded bigotry; to propagate that religion across the world is cultural imperialism; and to claim that one is right is a rationalization of the fact that one is a Christian because one happened to be born in Bristol rather than Bahrain or Bombay.

This attitude has been expressed more formally by theologians such as John Hick and Paul Knitter.[7] Hick pleads for a new 'Copernican revolution' in religious thought: God must now replace Christ as its centre. This immediately opens the way for other faiths to be seen as growing out of experiences of the one God in different cultural settings. Because they were largely isolated from one another in the so-called 'golden age of religious activity' (*c.* 900 BC–*c.* AD 200), they developed the diversity in practice and belief that we encounter today.

For these theologians, God is truly encountered in Christ, but not *only* in Christ. The language of incarnation and the exclusive claims about him were not part of his own message, but were the early disciples' attempts to explain his significance because he had saved them. Further, the doctrine of the uniqueness of Christ is morally indefensible, not just because it consigns the majority of humankind to hell, but because it holds that God has revealed himself definitively in a white male. Such presumption has led to racism, sexism and, since Christ died at the instigation of the Jews, anti-Semitism.

the relativity of relativism

One problem with the position of these theologians is that it seems to take competing claims about truth and turn them into relative beliefs. One religion says that Jesus Christ is the only way; another that Muhammad is the last great prophet. Both these claims cannot be true, yet relativists are asking the majority of the world's population to abandon such cherished beliefs for the soup of relativism without arguing them out. More importantly, how relative is the relativism of these theologians? Where is the intellectual high ground which enables them to look down on all the religions of the world and judge them in this way? One suspects that it amounts to no more than the cultural and philosophical attitudes of the West at the end of the twentieth century. Paul Knitter, in fact, traces his position back to Ernst Troeltsch's historical relativism (the contention that any revelation which is historical must be relative), and actually quotes Hans-Georg Gadamer's hermeneutics as a basis for his view.[8]

Lesslie Newbigin points out another important inconsistency in this presentation. Even the most ardent relativist excludes some viewpoints as unacceptable. These scholars do not accept Hitler's ideas of ultimate reality and his sense of divine mission as one expression of truth among others, or even as valid for the German people in the 1930s. But in order to make such judgments, we need a solid, supracultural basis. Relativism in religion seems to mean accepting the values and worldviews of only some people. But on what basis?[9]

orthodox exclusivism

In the face of a plurality of religions, the church has traditionally asserted the uniqueness of Jesus Christ as the only Saviour of the world, and the response of faith to the message of the gospel as the only way to receive the grace of salvation. 'Salvation is found in no-one else, for there is no other name under heaven given to men by which we must be saved' (Acts 4:12).

This view too has had its weighty advocates. Karl Barth, for instance, entitled the relevant part of his *Church Dogmatics* 'The Revelation of God as the Abolition of Religion'. For him, every religion, even Christianity in so far as it is a religion, is false. Only the revelation of God in Christ is true. All religions are 'unbelief' because they attempt to understand God outside his exclusive revelation in Jesus.[10] The Roman Catholic expression of this exclusivism has been that 'outside the church there is no salvation'. The Reformers agreed with this, but defined the church as wherever the Word of God is truly preached and the sacraments faithfully administered. This view of Christian uniqueness has been a great driving force behind the missionary movement in evangelicalism. As Howard Lindsell said of everyone in the world, 'If they die without knowledge of Christ, they perish.'[11]

inclusive ideas

This exclusivist consensus has now broken down within the Roman Catholic Church since the Second Vatican Council and within the World Council of Churches since about 1966. On 28 October 1965, Vatican 2 adopted the document *Nostra Aetate*, which redefined the Catholic Church's attitude to other faiths. The most significant passage for this redefinition in the documents coming out of Vatican 2, however, is in *Lumen Gentium* (1964). It reaffirmed the first principle that salvation was granted only through the merits of Christ, but it dropped the second by affirming that his saving merits could be applied to those outside the church.[12]

Karl Rahner, one of the most influential of recent Catholic theologians, developed this idea in his concept of 'anonymous Christians'. Those without the knowledge of Christ are bound into a cultural system which includes their religion. Non-Christians must work out their salvation within that situation and therefore within their religion. Faithfulness of intention becomes the signal for God to apply Christ's merits to them, through, as it were, the sacraments of their non-Christian religion. Thus Christ saves them without their knowing that it is by his merits. Rahner held that such a way of salvation is less likely, less sure and less complete than by consciously coming to Christ, and it disappears altogether as a possible way of salvation as soon as individuals hear of Christ for themselves.[13]

Rahner's view has been criticized as a messy non-solution. It does not seem to take account of the biblical statements that other religions are idolatry; it weakens the need for conversion which is so prominent in the New Testament, and it hardly satisfies the relativists either. To say that other religions are secretly efficacious because of the work of Christ (the efficacy of which they deny) is to adopt a very condescending attitude towards them.

some new evangelical thinking

A significant body of evangelical writers have made similar attempts to come to terms with the new situation without abandoning salvation only through Christ. These include Sir Norman Anderson, Charles Kraft, Clark Pinnock and Peter Cotterell.[14] They see the traditional exclusivist view as incompatible with the character of God. The view that God condemns the vast majority of the men, women and children he has made to an eternity in hell, without any possibility of their avoiding it, is hard to square with his love and justice. It may seem to our limited thinking that the Bible teaches such mass condemnation, but, to quote Faber's hymn, 'the love of God is broader than the measure of man's mind'. Most evangelicals believe that the triumph of God in this world requires many more to be saved than lost, but few claim to know how it will come about. Indeed, if the last two thousand years are anything to go by, it does not seem likely that this will come about through the missionary activity of the church. Even the great modern missionary movement, which has spread the church into almost every country in the world and has had large successes in black Africa and parts of Asia, has made a very small impact on the great religions.

The question of the way God regards non-Christians or pre-Christians is further raised by the evidence that God works in and through them. Cotterell gives the example of an African prophet who foretold the coming of missionaries and the gospel to Ethiopia. As a result, when missionaries did arrive with the gospel, many came to Christ. But the forerunner died just before the gospel came. Cotterell asks, 'Where is he now?'

These scholars believe that it is only through the merits of Christ that anyone can be saved. But they suggest that, in certain circumstances, individuals can be saved without a personal, conscious decision to trust Christ as Saviour and Lord. Pinnock points out that most evangelicals already believe this to be possible in at least two cases. First, those Old Testament saints who will be in heaven (not all of whom were Jews) can be there only because of the sacrifice of Christ for their sins. They put their faith in a saving God, not knowing what we know about Christ and his death. Secondly, most evangelicals who practise infant baptism hold that God is gracious to deceased infants who are baptized in Christ, and even to those who are not. Most evangelicals who practise only believer's baptism are usually as generous as C. H. Spurgeon, the great Baptist preacher, who believed that somehow the merits of Christ are applied to all who die before they are old enough to understand the gospel.

Having accepted the principle that Christ's merits can in certain circumstances be applied to individuals without conscious faith in him, what of those in the world today who have never heard of Christ? Are they not in the same position as Old Testament people? For them, the gospel has not yet come. Do they deserve to be judged more harshly than those who lived before Christ? Does our Lord's prayer on the cross, 'Father, forgive them, for they do not know what they are doing' (Lk. 23:34), imply a divine attitude in such cases?

It is difficult to assess these ideas because so little is said in Scripture on the issue. A number of passages imply that conscious faith in Christ is the only way to salvation (*e.g.* Jn. 3:16ff.; Acts 4:12). In the light of the above arguments, the advocates of this theory usually see these passages as referring to those who have had the gospel presented to them. They would also argue for the importance of general revelation (Acts 14:15ff.; 17:22ff.; Rom. 1:18ff.) and of the enlivening and illuminating work of the Word (= Jesus) in all people (Jn. 1:1–14).

These views have not found much acceptance among evangelicals because it is believed that they undermine the missionary task. The problem has to be faced. Many, such as Hudson Taylor, have been driven to mission by their certainty that those without a knowledge of Christ are lost. The advocates of the 'evangelical inclusivist' position of Cotterell and others would reply that the greatest motive for mission has always been love for God and his kingdom, and a desire to bring people to a conscious knowledge of Christ, since only then will they be able to live a fully human and meaningful life here and now.

Whichever view we hold, or whether we are agnostic on this issue, it seems clear that the church's task is to preach the gospel to everyone in this world. God is the one who decides the fate of each person.

choosing Christ amid the world religions

We must now come back to our central issue: how we can reasonably choose Christ amid the diversity of religions on offer today. It would be easy to justify that choice by saying that Christ is the best of all the 'products' offered in the religious supermarket. But as well as demeaning

Christ, this is almost certainly not how most of us came to decide to follow him. Some had a Christian home which helped them to faith in Christ. Others were impressed by the life of a Christian friend, and began to ask the questions which led them along the path of faith. Very few, if any, have come to faith in Christ by setting out the various religions on the kitchen table and deciding which one is best.

In this context, the Bible talks about *election*. Our choice of Christ depended on his prior choice of us. That choice was made before creation, and we were given to Christ before he came to die for sin. It is a difficult doctrine to square with some assertions in Scripture about our responsibility to believe in Christ when the gospel is presented to us. Yet it is the only way to avoid pride in having made a good consumer choice. Why am I a Christian? Because I was born in the right place? Because I was clever enough to see the advantages when others did not? Christians prefer to answer: because of God, his choice and his work.

Having said that, the decision to place Christ at the centre of our life is eminently reasonable. Christians have a faith which meets the needs of human beings. It sometimes speaks of mysteries, but it goes a long way towards explaining the world. It brings relief from the universal burden of sin and guilt and gives life a valid purpose. It provides the motive and power to serve the world, allows us to die a good death, and brings us into the presence of God himself, now and for ever.

the Bible and the Christian

Christ, the centre of our life, is mediated to us through the Bible.

Christians have a tradition of believing that applying the Bible is easier than it really is; that the Bible is a sort of systematic textbook with an index, rather like a schoolbook on chemistry. All we need to do is to look up the subject, go to the passage indicated and there find instruction on what to do or believe. But, of course, it is not that simple.

The orthodox doctrine of Scripture states that the Bible makes three claims about itself. First, the Bible records God's self-revelation. It tells the story of God's acts and records their explanation by the prophets and apostles. Especially, it is the story of God's great act in Jesus Christ. Secondly, God supervised the understanding and recording of that revelation. In other words, he 'breathed' or inspired the Scriptures. Thirdly, it follows from these two affirmations that the Bible has the authority of God's Word. As such, it may be presumed to contain all that God desires us to know for our faith and our lives.

Two important developments in scholarship have been regarded by some as a threat to this doctrine, and by others as a means to enrich our understanding. The nineteenth century explored the implications of the Bible's humanity, and the late twentieth those of the cultural distance between the reader and the original documents.

the humanity of the Bible

Muslims believe that the Qur'an was dictated word for word to Muhammad. Mormons believe that the Book of Mormon was discovered engraved on gold plates. Christians, by contrast, believe that the Bible was written by human beings who used their minds and skills in the process. So, said eighteenth-century Enlightenment scholars, we can examine the Bible as a set of human documents.

In the nineteenth and twentieth centuries new critical methods were developed with this in view. Source criticism posited written sources behind the biblical documents as they have come down to us. Julius Wellhausen held that the Pentateuch had been built up out of four main sources, each with its own characteristics. Christian Weisse concluded that the writers of Matthew, Mark and Luke used an early version of Mark to which they added their own material; Matthew and Luke also used a compilation of Jesus' sayings. Form criticism looked at the genre of each literary unit in the gospels and tried to work back to its original historical context (which was regarded as being in the life of the early church rather than in the ministry of Jesus). Redaction criticism asked why each gospel writer had put his book together in the way he did, and what this tells us about his special theological concerns.[15]

Some scholars not only investigated the books of the Bible as historical documents, but regarded them as no more than that. This led evangelical scholars to reaffirm the doctrine of inspiration and define it more precisely, using such terms as 'propositional revelation', 'verbal inspiration', 'infallibility' and 'inerrancy'. They have also taken on board the humanity of the Scriptures and have entered into the task of modern biblical criticism in the search to explain how this works.

The doctrine of Scripture has been the area of greatest debate for evangelicals in the last 150 years. They are still divided on the precise meaning and application of the terms used to describe Scripture. 'Infallibility' is the older word and signifies 'entire trustworthiness'. 'Inerrancy' signifies 'total truthfulness', 'no mistakes'. But what is an error? Does infallibility require Christians to believe in seven literal days of creation in Genesis, to harmonize the chronologies of all four gospels, to accept that

David wrote all the psalms that bear his name, or to maintain that Moses alone wrote the Pentateuch, including the account of his own death?[16]

Nowadays, with the downgrading of Enlightenment concerns and disputes, another debate has taken centre stage: how we can come to terms with the cultural distance between the writers and the modern readers of Scripture. Hermeneutics is the new controversy.

hermeneutics

As we saw earlier, because of the impact of Gadamer and those who followed him, hermeneutics has become a vital area of current philosophy. Gadamer emphasizes the distance between the writer of a text (whether legal, literary or biblical) and its reader and interpreter. The writer is embedded in a specific culture with all its presuppositions, which the reader cannot fully enter. The reader, in turn, comes to the text with pre-understandings based on his own culture and experiences. These pre-understandings, the tradition of which he is a part, limit his understanding of the text. They create a horizon beyond which he cannot see. Nevertheless, his own pre-understanding of the issue makes him ask questions of the text. As he asks these questions, he becomes aware of their inadequacy, and, as a result of his encounter with the text, he is able to frame better questions. As he takes those better questions back to the text, this 'hermeneutical circle' becomes an upward spiral of engagement with the text. The horizon of the text moves towards the reader, and his horizon approaches that of the text. Eventually the horizons fuse; the text speaks in a relevant way with transforming effect. Because the context in which the interpretation takes place varies, the text will speak in different ways to each different situation. The one text therefore gives rise to many messages.

the new biblical hermeneutic

Ernst Fuchs and Gerhard Ebeling applied this dynamic to the Scriptures in what has come to be known as 'the new hermeneutic'.[17] While they emphasize the cultural distance between writer and interpreter, they are more concerned with what goes on in front of the text than with what goes on behind it (to use Paul Ricoeur's phrase). In other words, they focus on what is happening in the reader.

They make some points which we need to hear. For instance, they emphasize that there is no such thing as 'presuppositionless exegesis'. We bring to the Scriptures not only our own cultural and personal prejudices, but also our church's traditional interpretation and the doctrinal framework into which a given passage must be made to fit. The hermeneutical circle helps to bring us closer to the Scriptures only if we allow them to judge us in this respect. We must avoid the old attitude to the Bible which saw the reader as the subject examining the scriptural text as the object. Rather, we must become the object examined by and confronted by the text.

Despite this positive contribution, the new hermeneutic undermines an evangelical view of the Bible. It carries with it no understanding of the Bible as conveying supracultural revelation. Instead, it regards truth as individual and personal. 'We should accept as true', says Fuchs, 'only that which we acknowledge as valid for our own person.'[18]

dealing with cultural distance

When a Christian at the end of the twentieth century sits down with a cup of coffee and a Bible, what is going on? The texts she reads were written at least 1,800 years ago, and some are 3,000 years old. God's revelation took place at specific times and in particular places, and so each document belongs to its own culture. Moreover, the Christian reader brings all her own cultural and personal assumptions to the task.

culturally specific Scripture

The culturally specific nature of the Bible is evident in commands which deal with customs. Five times in the New Testament we are told to greet one another with a holy kiss, a sign of affection in the culture of the time (as it is in many countries today). There is no need for Christians in all cultures to follow this command literally; rather, the principle behind the command can be expressed in a culturally appropriate way. The Anglo-Saxon equivalent is the handshake: boring but much safer. A similar attitude should be taken to Jesus' command that his disciples should wash one another's feet (Jn. 13). Here is an expression of humility and love suitable for a situation of open sandals and dusty roads. We must express the same qualities in our own culture.

But the culturally specific nature of the Bible is evident not just in commands, but in the use of language. Metaphors, for instance, vary from culture to culture. Jesus called Herod a fox. With our pre-understanding we would take that to mean that Herod was sly and cunning. In the culture of the time, however, it indicated treachery.

When I was lecturing in Africa, my students and I looked at Paul's analogy of the church as the bride of Christ (Eph. 5:22–33). They had a rich cultural background from which to interpret this passage. For instance, just as men in their culture paid a high bride price for their wives, so Christ has paid a high price for the church. From my cultural background, I saw marriage as primarily to do with companionship, so the text spoke to me of the fellowship I can have with Christ. Paul was not majoring on either point. He was probably correcting a tendency in his own culture to see the husband's headship as privilege rather than as duty.

Some scholars are presently questioning whether we should read the books of the Bible only from within the literary conventions of our own time and culture. It seems more faithful to recognize that the writers wrote in the style of their own era. The gospel of John, for instance, is structured around some key miracles which interact with clusters of relevant sayings of Jesus. Our literary convention would be to write more chronologically; but that does not make John's approach wrong.

There are even deeper levels of cultural specificity (which we shall explore in the section on doctrinal diversity at the beginning of chapter 4), but enough has been said to show that, because revelation is historical, it takes on the character of the culture into which it came.

culture and authority

Yet we must not regard the Bible as so culturally specific that it can no longer be universally authoritative. Human beings at their deepest level are remarkably consistent, which is why the texts of Homer, Shakespeare and Endo can speak so powerfully to us on universal themes such as love, betrayal, honour and suffering. One of the problems of applying modern hermeneutical ideas to the Bible is that the text is not just a human document. The Bible is revelation, with God as its supracultural originator and applier. Jesus was both human and divine, and his humanity does not rule out his divinity. In a similar way, the Bible is human and therefore culturally specific, but this does not mean that it cannot also transcend culture as God's Word.

Nevertheless, it is vital to recognize the distance between the cultural forms of that revelation and our own cultural ways of thinking and acting. If we do not, we simply read into the text what we have already assumed that it is saying. Reading Scripture then becomes a way of reinforcing our own community's beliefs, lifestyle and identity. We are using the Bible as a theological comfort blanket.

The way out of this predicament is through study. Only when we get as deeply as possible into the mind and background of the writer are we able to let the Word speak freshly. Much has been written about the impossibility of this aim. We can acknowledge that we shall never entirely understand, and that some texts remain a mystery for this very reason. But we need to get as close to the writer as possible, in order to empathize, to understand where he is coming from and why he says things the way he does.

We are also given the Holy Spirit to help us. He inspired the writings in the first place and it is he who gives us discernment in reading. Two cautions are necessary. First, he is not a substitute for the use of our minds. He guides our minds, so understanding the Bible is not a question of study *or* prayer, but of both. Secondly, the fact that he gives us spiritual wisdom does not mean that Christians will never disagree about any minor point. Plainly, we do! But the Spirit is there to teach us about Christ: the great facts of his person and work and their significance for us. If I may say it reverently, God does not bother too much about all the little things we so often get hung up on as Christians.

the bias of the reader

We come to the text, then, with a tradition, a pre-understanding, through which we look at the words. It includes our own cultural viewpoints. For instance, our modern materialistic culture finds it hard to accept the supernaturalism of the Bible because we are used to the idea of cause and effect within a closed system. This is the way science has taught us to look at the world. When we encounter miracles, angels and devils in the Bible, therefore, some disbelieve these accounts, some ignore them, and some accept them without integrating this element into their thinking and life.

We have already seen that we bring an additional tradition to the Bible: that of the way our own church or denomination has understood the text in the past. We have a doctrinal frame of reference within which we read the Bible and into which we must fit each passage. This is not always easy, because the framework has been constructed not only out of the Scriptures, but also out of historical circumstances and controversies. For instance, English evangelicals in the last 150 years have mostly been teetotallers. Yet Jesus turned water into wine. Some have explained this by maintaining that it was non-alcoholic wine. (After all, the master of the feast called it the best wine, and the best wine is non-alcoholic!)

Deeper distortions emerge when we read the Scriptures with different views of grace or salvation. For instance, in the first four centuries after Christ many theologians read the Bible with a particular view of matter

– that it was intrinsically evil and alien to God. This made it difficult for them to understand the incarnation, in which the Son of God took a human body. It also encouraged the ascetic excesses of the early monastic movement, as if holiness depended on inflicting pain on one's own body. To take an example from our own day, liberation theologians tell us that in the West, salvation has been seen primarily in personal terms, because of our individuality and tendency to relegate religion to the realm of personal rather than public truth. Once society is seen as important to God, and therefore an equally valid arena for religious judgments, one is able to agree with liberation theology that love that is not political is not love. And so we could go on.

bias in biblical scholarship

It is, of course, easier to see other people's presuppositions than our own, and this is true of biblical scholars too. They have been better at describing the biblical writers' cultural background than their own. Old and New Testament scholarship has often operated on the basis of a false objectivity. The 'science' of exegesis has been assigned to the university, as though the churches cannot be trusted with the task because their faith commitment distorts scholarly impartiality. Fortunately, this attitude is dying fast. The new hermeneutic asserts that no-one comes empty-handed to the text. Presuppositions are all the more dangerous for being unrecognized. We all have faith commitments, whether they be to Christ, to a materialistic worldview or to Enlightenment attitudes.

Biblical scholars have also failed to serve us well by assuming that their task is more a matter of technique and method than of empathy. Their minute examination of the text and its cultural background has too often been regarded as the goal of the process, and as providing us with enough to understand the Scriptures – as if one could appreciate a Beethoven sonata by taking apart the piano. Hebrew exegesis and ancient Near Eastern studies have a place in the interpretation of (for instance) Psalm 73, but the best interpreter will be one who has gone through a spiritual experience similar to that of the writer. Greek exegesis can be done by a schoolchild. Understanding the New Testament requires an experienced Christian.

One other matter needs to be mentioned, and it comes out of this very point. When empathy occurs – when horizons fuse – then a true encounter with the text takes place, and, through the text, with God. At that moment, we need to obey, to act. Indeed, we shall never arrive at that moment until it is our intention to obey. As Jesus said, 'If anyone chooses to do God's will, he will find out ...' (Jn 7:17). Obedience then becomes part of our hermeneutical circle, and predisposes us to understand more. This too is the work of the Holy Spirit.

positive enculturizing

It would be easy to give the impression that the reader's culture is a hindrance to understanding. But it is not so. Every reading requires a positive fusing of the Bible and our own culture. There is a way of reading the Bible that is relevant in our own situation. We have already seen examples in the reapplication of Paul's command to greet one another with a kiss, and Jesus' command to wash one another's feet. We must look to apply the supracultural norm or principle, stripped of the cultural trappings that belonged to its biblical setting, but clothed with new forms appropriate to our own culture. Thus we shake hands warmly and get the other person's shopping. Later, we shall see how this applies in various ethical and theological situations.

conclusions

1. *We need to recognize the unique authority of the Bible.* It mediates Christ to us. Submission to Christ and centring our life around Christ therefore require a corresponding attitude to the Bible. As people who are 'in Christ', we shall use the Bible to construct our values and attitudes. C. H. Spurgeon once described a Puritan author by saying that his very blood was 'bibline'. It will be enough that our thinking patterns are so.

2. *We need to understand the cultures in which the Word of God is embedded.* In John 4, Jesus meets a Samaritan woman at a well. We cannot fully grasp the meaning of the story until we understand something about Samaritans and Jews, their attitudes to each other, why the woman may have been at the well at that time of day, the society's rules about men conversing with women, and why Jesus sent her home to speak to her husband. A good commentary should tell us these things.

3. *To understand the Bible, we must understand ourselves.* We should recognize that our own presuppositions, gathered from our church, culture and personal experience, are operating every time we read the Bible. Understanding these will help us to be more faithful in extracting its meaning. Reading about our own society, and if possible some anthropology, will help us to understand where we are coming from.

4. *It is useful to read the Bible through the eyes of people with different interpretational frameworks.* Christians from Africa and the Middle East often

understand some parts of the Bible, such as the parables of Jesus, or the account of Abraham bargaining for land to bury Sarah, better than we do. Their cultural background is closer than ours to that of the text. Most commentary-writers have been men, but women often have a different and more faithful perspective on some passages, arising out of their experiences as women. Reading the commentaries of those believers who have a different theological or ecclesiastical background from our own is helpful.

5. *When we read the Bible, we must be open to change.* It is a costly thing to depart from a traditional viewpoint. It can affect our present circle of fellowship. If there is little tolerance of diversity in our Christian community, we may no longer be welcome if we do not follow its line in every interpretation. Yet we must maintain an openness to having our preconceptions judged by the Word of God.

6. *We must pray for the help of the Holy Spirit.* Evangelicals do not believe that tradition is supremely authoritative in the interpretation of the Bible, or that the Holy Spirit leads us without regard to the Bible. Rather, they hold that the Spirit is the true interpreter of the Word. He provides understanding of the message of God, he witnesses to its truth and, as the Bible is opened up in public preaching or private reading, he mediates Christ through the text.

7. *The history of the interpretation of a passage is valuable for us today.* We do not have to believe that biblical study prior to the Enlightenment is useless to the modern reader. The Holy Spirit has a history. We are justified in reading the Bible together with all the saints, and especially with the early Fathers and the Reformers. This both enriches our interpretation and safeguards us from major error.

8. *It is important to encourage expository preaching of the best kind.* There are many preachers of whom it can be said, 'Ten thousand thousand are their texts, but all their sermons one.' They do not delve sufficiently deeply or honestly into the texts, but use their chosen verses as pegs on which to hang the small number of ideas they already possess. Preachers must engage with the text sufficiently to allow it to broaden their horizon and rework their views and attitudes. Only then can they expound it to others.

9. *There is no point in reading if we do not intend to take action.* Uninvolved reading does not get to the truth. The Bible was written so that we might be saved, converted, made holy, and live as God's good servants. To read it impartially is to misread it.

10. *We need to recognize that differences among those who believe and trust the Bible are simply hermeneutical.* When we begin with the Scriptures as the

inspired and sufficient Word of God, we share the same foundation. Differences arise only as we try to discover its truth, extract it properly and apply it to our various situations. We owe one another the respect that comes from acknowledging that we share the same starting-point and the same aims.

In chapter 1 we looked at the diversity of our present society and the attitudes people take towards it. In chapter 2 we have explored how the Christian can handle diversity and make choices on the basis of Christ and the Bible. In the following chapters we move on to look at how this works out in four crucial areas: ethics (what we think is right), theology (what we are to believe), mission (how we should get involved in God's world), and unity (how we can react to the diversity of churches). In each case, our first task will be to understand the nature of the diversity that faces us and its origins. We shall then seek a way through it for those who delight in the centrality of Christ and the authority of Scripture.

3. ethics

We have glanced at the huge range of possibilities offered by today's pluralistic society. But not everything that is possible is right. We have noted how the specifics of situation or culture affect our choices. How then can our choices bow to the will of God? How do they relate to what is holy? We start by looking at how the diversity of ethical choice created by technology, culture and postmodern attitudes can be related to the Word of God. This will lead on to the question, 'What is it to be worldly today?'

Most moral choices are 'new'. Jane is a student. She needs to know whether to study on Sundays, how far to go with her boyfriend, how much she should spend on a new CD player, whether to attend the rave next Saturday, what sort of swimsuit to buy for the holidays and which candidate to vote for in the election. When she approaches an older Christian, she is told, 'Do what the Bible tells you to do.' But the Bible does not discuss bikinis and CD players. To her, the New Testament looks decidedly old. Peter knew nothing about the dilemmas of different methods of contraception. Jesus did not live in a democracy, and Paul told slaves to obey their masters.

technological distance

As we have seen, technology has been a massive engine for change in our society. As it creates new machines, so it creates new situations to which we must respond. The coming of the cinema divided Christians after the Second World War just as the use of some forms of music and media does today. The mass-volume printing-press which made newspapers cheap also created Sunday newspapers and so left Christians with another choice – to buy or not to buy. Cars give us more convenient travel but cause environmental damage. Mass-market publishing requires us to choose which books not to read. The invention of the cigarette means we must take a decision about smoking. All these issues are new in the sense that the technology which produced them was not available in Bible times. Therefore there are no specific commands or examples in the Scriptures to help us in our choices.

Medicine is another area of dramatic advance, creating new ethical choices. Contraception was known in Egypt in 1900 BC, but in the 1960s the 'pill' made it possible for human beings to have sex at any time without significant risk of pregnancy. This scientific advance, along with the increased reliability and convenience of other forms of contraception, created a revolution in our culture. Premarital and extramarital sex had been discouraged by the three fears of detection, infection and conception. Modern antibiotics made infection less dreaded, and modern contraceptives virtually eliminated the last fear. This breaking of the bond between sex and procreation has had radical implications for our ideas of family and marriage, and even of the purpose of sex. Roman Catholics have generally taken decisions collectively, and Rome has chosen against isolating sex from the possibility of procreation. Nowadays, Aids has given society back the fear of infection, but the new attitudes created by the sixties revolution have not changed.

More recently, scientists' ability to bring about *in vitro* fertilization and to manipulate embryos has handed us a whole new sheaf of choices. Artificial insemination by husband can be seen as merely overcoming a physical problem. Donor insemination, using the sperm of a donor when the husband is infertile, has been called adultery without the pleasure. *In vitro* fertilization creates 'spare' embryos. Medical technology now allows a man not only to choose a female lifestyle but also a 'female' body. At this stage we are not so much concerned to provide answers to these dilemmas as to note that technology has generated a bewildering diversity of new possibilities which require ethical choice.[1]

grey-area Christianity

How can we use the Bible in making such choices? Moral decisions seem to fall into three basic categories in relation to the Scriptures. There are acts which are clearly and specifically forbidden, such as adultery and murder. There are acts which are clearly commanded, such as love for one another, and prayer. In between is a grey area where there are no clear or precise commands because of the newness of the situation.

In such cases we take principles set out in the Bible, either in didactic passages or in specific biblical situations where we see them being worked out. We use these to decide the issue. Or, as discussed earlier, we extract the norm from the biblical cultural form and apply it to a new cultural situation. The technical term for this process is 'casuistry', although the fact that casuistry has often been used to get around the biblical norms altogether has given it a bad press. The reason Christians disagree in the grey area is that this process is messy and difficult, and a number of different conclusions may well be possible. Consider a few case studies.

The first is easy for most of us. To smoke or not is a choice offered to Christians today. We now have plenty of evidence that smoking damages the body. A principle in the Bible is that the body is a gift from God, to be looked after. Our bodies were created by the word of the Father, will be redeemed and made new by the work of the Son, and are indwelt by the Holy Spirit. Although smoking is not mentioned in the Bible, therefore, most Christians do not smoke.

The second is a little more complicated. In 1989, a leading army officer in Nigeria approached a Christian missionary asking for guidance on whether he should take part in a coup against the military dictatorship. He was a Christian himself. On the one hand, passages in the Bible told him to obey those who rule over us (and when Romans 13 was written, most of the civilized world was under a military dictatorship based in Rome). On the other hand, the evil of the present regime and the suffering it was causing were plain for all to see. His duty to God and his duty to his fellows seemed to be on opposing sides. Which biblical principle should he follow?

three theories

This is an old dilemma. Historically, three positions have been adopted in such situations.[2] First, Scottish Presbyterian John Murray (in *Principles of Conduct*, 1957) and others hold that the conflict of principles is not real. It cannot be, since God cannot require two conflicting things in one situation. Either we have misread the situation, or we can trust God's providence to show us a third way which avoids breaking either principle of Scripture. But the difficulty with this view is that third alternatives are not always available. In some obstetric cases, for instance, either the baby must die or the mother will die, and the doctor has to choose or both will die. Such conflicts are real, and it is very possible to sin by omission.

The Lutheran theologian Helmut Thielicke, secondly, says in his vast *Theological Ethics* (1951–64) that in cases when two moral absolutes conflict, we must choose the lesser evil. We cannot avoid sin, so we must choose the lesser sin. In the case of the Nigerian asked to join a coup, he is bound to fail in his duty either way, and must decide which is the lesser evil: disobedience to the government or lack of compassion towards the poor of his country. But this view also seems untenable. It suggests that sometimes our moral duty is to sin. If such moral conflicts are real and inevitable it also suggests that Christ must have sinned while on earth. Surely no situation can *oblige* Christians to sin.

The third position is that of Augustine. He acknowledges that conflicts are real. But in such cases we follow not the lesser evil, but the greater good. Some principles in Scripture are important enough to override others. Some attitudes are more important to God than others. It is better to love and please God than to love and please human beings. Jesus himself spoke of the greatest commandment and of the more important matters of the law (Mt. 22:37–40; 23:23). It is no sin to apply the most important principle in the circumstances. Sometimes we must inflict pain to save life, imprison someone to protect society, kill to defend the right. Our army officer needs to decide which is the most important principle in the situation, and that may depend on precisely what he is being asked to do.

In the light of this analysis, and by way of final illustration, is it ever permissible for Christians to tell a lie? The person who believes that principles never come into real conflict will say no. Those who hid Jews from the SS in the Second World War never needed to lie, and if they did, they sinned. Murray draws a distinction between lying and intentionally deceiving. A commander is not doing his job well unless he deceives his enemy regarding his intention. When we go out in the evening, we probably leave a light on to deceive would-be burglars. No Christian, however, is permitted to *speak* a deception, a lie. But drawing this distinction as a way out of the problem does not convince.

Alternatively, those who follow Augustine allow lying when a greater biblical principle requires it in the circumstances. A mother who lies to save her child from a murderer does not sin. The Hebrew midwives did not sin when they lied to avoid the death of the babies in Egypt, and Rahab did not sin when she lied to protect the spies.

situation ethics?

This method of applying different norms or commands to a new situation has certain disadvantages. First, as we have already seen, we sometimes have to choose which command we think is the most important – not an easy decision. Secondly, we are constantly in danger of legalism. Mark Twain spoke of 'a good man in the worst sense of the term'. Such a person sticks to the rules but does not show love. Situation ethics attempts to take proper notice of the situation in which we decide. It says that the question 'Is it right?' is always complicated and the answer always depends on the situation. This attempt to deal with the problem is no mere abstract theory, for we are likely to encounter similar views regularly in pubs, schools and college bars.

Joseph Fletcher, in his books *Situation Ethics* (1966) and *Moral Responsibility* (1967), put forward the idea that there are not many norms, but one supracultural norm, one universal law, and that is love. There are many principles and portions of wisdom which help us on the way, but, because every situation in which we have to make moral decisions is different, we have to work out what to do, in the midst of each situation, on the basis of what would be most loving. Only love is good in itself, and so every commandment can be broken for the sake of love.

Take a soldier who commits suicide rather than betray his fellows. For Fletcher, this is right because it is the most loving thing. Lies can be loving lies. Fletcher believes that even adultery could be the most loving course of action in a situation. He refers to a play, *The Rainmaker* by H. Richard Nash, in which a man sleeps with a woman not out of attraction, but to give her a sense of being a woman and to save her from spinsterhood. Her brother goes off to get his gun and take revenge, but is stopped by their father. 'Noah,' he says, 'you're so full of what's right that you can't see what's good.'[3]

This love is not a vague emotion. It is *agapē*, calculating love. It is, in fact, the equivalent of justice. Justice is simply love distributed, nothing else. As Paul says, 'Let no debt remain outstanding, except the continuing debt to love one another' (Rom. 13:8). It places on us the burden of hard thinking. Fletcher quotes the case of a Romanian doctor in a Second World War concentration camp. Because all pregnant women were incinerated, she performed 3,000 abortions. By killing 3,000 (who would have been killed anyway), she saved the life of 3,000, the most loving thing to be done in the situation.[4]

Fletcher deserves two cheers. He avoided legalism and pointed out the importance of the situation in an ethical decision. Yet he seems to ask for a level of calculation that is just not possible for sinful human beings. With our limited knowledge of the future, we may think that an action is the most loving, but it could well turn out to be a disaster. More often, our idea of what is loving is coloured, consciously or not, by our sinfulness or selfishness. We need some rules which tell us in advance what is right and wrong, even though, in unusual circumstances, one rule may be more important than the other. We need Christ to tell us, 'If you love me, you will obey what I command' (Jn. 14:15).[5]

cultural ethics

The discussion so far has assumed a modern rather than a postmodern attitude. The Enlightenment, when it overthrew ethics as established by the authority of religious doctrines and pronouncements, did not abandon the idea of ethical absolutes, but sought to establish them by reason. John

Locke held that moral principles are just as self-evident to reason as are mathematical axioms. Everyone knows that murder and adultery are wrong, just as everyone knows that two plus two equals four. Even Christian theologians of the Enlightenment, while believing that revelation was a quicker process, held that Christian moral principles could eventually be shown to be true by reason. The skeleton in the ethical closet, however, is cultural relativism. Different cultures seem to reach different conclusions about what is right and wrong.

Fletcher's approach is typical of Enlightenment thought because it is fiercely individualistic. The individual must decide what is right or wrong. But this is not in fact what happens. Consciously or not, one's community or culture decides. There is no such thing as a view from nowhere, where each of us looks out on the world from the standpoint of his or her individual culture. In today's intellectual climate, therefore, the old individualism in ethics is giving way to communitarianism in one form or another. The culture and values of a community have an important role in ethical decisions, whether they be the values of a tribe in Irian Jaya, attitudes within a modern eastern society such as Japan's, or the middle-class mindset of many English churches.

defining sin

There is no doubt that culture affects which particular actions we regard as sins.

Take the issue of female modesty. When western missionaries first went to Africa, they were horrified to see women naked from the waist up. It was 'immodest'. Later, those same women who had covered up for the sake of the missionaries were horrified when the female missionaries followed the new British fashion and wore skirts above the ankles, even occasionally above the knees. It was 'immodest'. Christians from each culture accepted the requirement of modesty (1 Tim. 2:9–10; *cf.* 1 Pet. 3:3–5), but their culture dictated the content of the word. Such a shift in definition is easy to see not just in crossing from one culture to another, but also as a culture changes. Western society has dramatically changed its definition of modesty in the last hundred years. Even within one contemporary culture, each cultural frame defines modesty differently. Modesty on the beach is different from modesty in church.

Paul in Ephesians tells children to obey their parents. In many cultures, children remain children as long as their parents are alive. A fifty-year-old man will still obey his seventy-year-old father. In modern western culture, we generally see sons and daughters ceasing to be children when they grow up and leave home. We say to a rebellious son, 'While you are in my house, you will go to church like the rest of us.' The implication is, 'After that, it's your responsibility; you are no longer a child.' When is a child not a child? That decision is vital for applying the command. Yet society rather than the Bible seems to be taking that decision for us.

Applying the commandment 'You shall not steal' entails a definition of personal property which varies with society and ideology. It varies geographically. Many cultures do not regard picking an occasional fruit from another's tree when one is hungry as stealing. But most English people would. In the last few centuries we have developed the concept of intellectual property. Because income and livelihoods depend upon authorship or composition, books, articles and musical works are copyrighted and their content can be stolen. No such idea was present in the sixteenth century, when fellow Reformers and rival publishing houses regularly issued editions of one another's work. Nowadays, even hymns and worship songs are copyrighted, and churches which want to reproduce them, for instance on OHP transparencies, must pay for the privilege – a 'capitalist' situation which Christians in other cultures find hard to accept.

when is a scripture relevant?

A second, and closely related, way in which culture varies the expression of our morality is that a culture has its own idea of which commands are relevant to specific situations. Many Christians in non-western cultures believe that their brothers and sisters in the West transgress the fifth commandment ('Honour your father and your mother') when they put their aged relatives in old people's homes. Christians in western countries generally believe that polygamy is a transgression of the seventh commandment ('You shall not commit adultery'). In both cases, the perceptions are inadequate and simplistic.

Polygamists operate from a cultural understanding of marriage which sometimes clashes with the western view more than with the biblical view. After all, some of the greatest friends of God were polygamists, and their work underlies some parts of the Bible. Westerners often regard lust as the motive for polygamy, whereas it more commonly arises from kindness to a dead brother's widow or even to the first wife, or from a desire for status in the community. Africans, looking at old people's homes in the West, rarely appreciate the complicated nature of the decision taken by the older person's children in a mobile society characterized by nuclear families, or that the home may indeed be the way to honour the parent at that time with the care that he or she needs.

The issue of the relevance of different commands is never-ending. As already mentioned, today we have to decide whether the seventh commandment is relevant to donor insemination.

There are occasions in the New Testament when ethical principles are applied in different ways in different situations. Josef Blank[6] shows how Jesus' command to his followers to leave home and sell all they had was appropriate for the itinerant disciples, but was not insisted upon for later city Christians, at least after the Jerusalem experiment in communal ownership. Indeed, Timothy is enjoined to command the rich in the congregation, not to sell all they have, but to be rich in good deeds (1 Tim. 6:17–19). Paul refused to circumcise Titus in one situation (Gal. 2:1–5), but circumcised Timothy in another (Acts 16:1–3).

the power of church culture

A third factor influencing our decisions about what is right and wrong is the power of the cultural situation, sometimes, to swamp biblical evidence. Just such a case is the belief that it is sinful to drink alcohol. This teaching is strongest within a particular cultural group in the church. It is geographically contained within the English- (and some German-) speaking countries, historically contained within the last 200 years, and religiously contained mostly within the Protestant dissenting churches.[7] The existence of these cultural boundaries does not tell us whether this position is right or wrong, but it must make us cautious. Clearly there is a cultural factor at work here. Christians in the Latin countries of southern Europe rarely take a total-abstinence position unless they have been strongly influenced by northern European or North American views. Martin Luther was fond of his beer, John Calvin kept a good wine cellar, and the English Reformation could be said to have started in the White Horse Inn in Cambridge over glasses of ale.

Very few, if any, New Testament scholars would contend that Jesus was a total abstainer or that he taught his disciples to be so. John the Baptist abstained from wine as a Nazirite, but Jesus came eating and drinking, so much so that he was called a drunkard by the Pharisees (Lk. 7:33–34). The memorial supper which he ordained for his disciples included the drinking of wine (Lk. 22:17–18). In one well-known incident, Jesus actually made wine himself, which was distributed to the wedding guests (Jn. 2:1–10). There is no evidence that any of this involved non-alcoholic wine. Jesus was not embarrassed to use vineyards as pictures of God's kingdom (Mt. 21:33–41), or to speak of himself as a vine (Jn. 15:1–8). It seems that he stood firmly in the Old Testament tradition which condemned drunkenness but saw wine as one of God's good gifts. The early church seems to have followed the same line: the New Testament letters condemn drunkenness and require church leaders to be not given to *much* wine (Gal. 5:19–21; Eph. 5:18; 1 Tim. 3:3, 8; Tit. 1:7).

How then did the idea that drinking wine was a sin swamp this biblical evidence among those who take the Bible as the authority for their lives? It is likely that the total-abstinence position arose among Christians in Victorian England and pre-Prohibition North America as they saw the great damage alcoholism was doing at that time. This was a complex situation involving great social evils which drove people to drink. It may well have been the wisest Christian response at that time simultaneously to encourage abstinence and to tackle the social evils. This decision, arising from a particular historical situation, was then read back into the Bible and eventually, for many Christians, became the only way to read and apply Scripture on this issue.

what is cultural and what is unchanging?

Some readers may be alarmed at the thought of allowing our cultural situation to dictate the way we apply the moral principles and commands of the Bible. It is clearly possible in this process to set aside the commands altogether. As we have seen, it is sometimes helpful to explore the original intention of the author of a given part of Scripture and then translate it into our own culture. But this does not always solve the problem. How do we know, for instance, whether Paul intended to enjoin a particular form of modesty for women at all times and everywhere, or just in the situation he was addressing? Was he aware of the difference between these two intentions?

Sometimes an example or piece of advice in Scripture is clearly flagged as a custom. Leah, as the elder daughter, had to be married before Rachel. This is described as 'our custom' (Gn. 29:26), and no-one considers it relevant to western families today. Another factor which helps is that a command often has in mind the judgment of society as well as the judgment of God. In 1 Timothy, obedient children are important for the way the world perceives their father, an elder in the church. Modesty is important for the way the world perceives the Christian woman. To that extent, the cultural practice must be taken into account. Yet there is more than one reason for modesty in dress. Regardless of how the world judges the Christian woman, she should not dress in such a way as to tempt men to sin.

The question is still not entirely answered. Missionaries have struggled with this issue for hundreds of years, and the struggle is just as prominent in western churches. Young people are often seen by 'churchy' middle-class Christians as transgressing the Bible when really they are offending against the conservative values of the older people's culture. As we have already seen, the illumination of the Holy Spirit and the help of Christians from different cultures enable us to work out how to apply Scripture. We need one another in this task, and must be gracious to one another when we disagree.

postmodern ethics

Many today would see western society as being in a late stage of an ethical process of emancipation – from ethics. We have seen that in premodern society in the West, no real separation was made between usefulness, truth, beauty and morality. Life as a whole was a unity and was as God willed it. To exercise choice was to be wrong. It was to say no to the *status quo* ordained by God. To be right was not a matter of choice, but of following the customary way of life.

Eventually, the power of tradition waned and individuals defined themselves by personal choices. Categories of rightness were created that broke the unity of thought and distinguished between the political, the beautiful, the true and the moral. Society set off down the pluralistic road as different values were chosen by individuals and groups. The power of the church to define morality weakened. But society could not be allowed to fall apart. A morally plural society would be unstable. This realization gave rise to the typically modern search for a universal ethic which all decent human beings could agree on, and which could be taught to all and reinforced by 'just' laws.

the failure of Enlightenment ethics

The conclusion that this project is impossible is the starting-point of the postmodern attitude to ethics (just as the conclusion that the Enlightenment search for universal truth is impossible became the starting-point for postmodern philosophy). This development has been fuelled by the rapidly changing social situation in the West. Change has been so fast that the older generation and the younger generation seem to share little common ground. Globalization has added to the break-up by making us aware of the vast array of cultures with their contradictory ethical codes.

Alasdair MacIntyre helps us to appreciate the depth of confusion left by this failure of the Enlightenment project in ethics. Imagine, he says, a world in which the natural sciences are rejected by society: books and laboratories are destroyed, science teaching is banned. Years later a positive attitude to science returns, but all that is left are fragments of truth, results rather than the way they were arrived at. People would sit in the cafés and argue about the merits of relativity or Euclidean geometry without a basis for either. 'What would appear to be rival and competing premises for which no further argument could be given would abound.'[8]

This is the ridiculous situation we find ourselves in with regard to ethics today. We have swept away the basis, the reasons why something is right or wrong, and are left to argue fatuously about opinions. From this point of departure, the impossibility of the 'modern' ethical enterprise, flow two distinct streams.

First, there are those (such as Michel Foucault) who speak of the death of the ethical idea. People can now be emancipated from any rules, principles or duties outside of themselves. Self-sacrifice is no longer legitimate. Individuals go for 'the good life', limited only by their tolerance of others who go about it in a different way. This, of course, is no mere philosophical theory, but the *de facto* practice of many in society today.

The other stream (seen, for instance, in Zygmunt Bauman) is more thoughtful. It too believes that we are at the end of 'an ethics that is universal and objectively founded'. Morality can no longer be predicted or guided by rules, but this is actually a step *towards* morality. It frees us to make personal, responsible, moral choices. The root cause of universal, or at least national, moral codes was the desire to impose order from the top down. The leaders and legislators decided what was good and imposed it on the people, thus stifling their moral life by denying them choice. The powers that be used morality for their own, often immoral, ends.[9]

Christians must admit, with indignation, that such manipulation goes on in society. One clear example was the popular justification for the 1991 Gulf War. Iraq's Saddam Hussein invaded Kuwait, and the West or 'free world' joined forces to drive him out. Political rhetoric commended the war to us in the name of freedom and self-determination for the Kuwaiti people. It was an open question, however, whether the West would have come to the rescue of Kuwait if the country's main export had been bananas rather than oil. Some pointed out that religious freedom in Saddam's Iraq was greater than in Kuwait, where Christians were not even allowed to hold services. Christians should not argue for a return to *official* ethical norms. They should ask people to obey God and to distinguish between the biblical and the official, despite the rhetoric.

what is right is not relative

The complete denial of universal ethical norms is not, of course, an option for Christians, however much the concept has been abused by the powerful. If the negative side of ethical relativism says that there are no universal ethical norms, then the converse, positive side says that every moral code is equally valid. Relativism leads to neutralism. Logically, that would lead us to accept that the Nazis' attitude to the Jews may well have been right for them. The Bosnian war has thrown up atrocities by both sides. A press cutting shows a twelve-year-old girl shot by a sniper in Sarajevo. She was not killed indiscriminately, although that too would have been a sin. She was picked out in the sights of a rifle, and someone pulled the trigger. To deny the universal category of wrong in the face of such an act is an absurdity. It also goes against much anthropological evidence; the vast majority of cultures across the world would condemn such a murder.

Above all, relativism takes no account of revelation. As Christians we want to please our God, to follow Christ. In order to do so, we need to know what pleases God, and to be shown Christ so that we can follow him. It may not be easy, but it is the Christian's task and sincere pleasure to find the will of God and do it. If we are to be holy as God is holy, we need this reference point outside ourselves, on the basis of which we can make moral choices and against which we can measure our actions.

the individual and the church

In much recent Christian ethics, the fragmentation of truth from the universal to the local has switched the emphasis away from brave individuals who battle to apply universal truth to their situation, and towards the Christian community as the body which legitimizes what is true and right. The Christian community thus provides the plausibility structure for truly Christian ethics. This emphasis on the faith community, the church, is in some ways merely a restatement of what the local Christian community has always done. It is perennially difficult for the individual Christian to apply God's norms to every specific situation. For most Christians, their church is the cultural subgroup which legitimizes their ethical decisions and provides social support for them.

Enlightenment individualism is still very much alive, however; indeed, there will always be individuals who choose differently from the group.

But the way we handle that diversity is crucial for the life of the church. There can be no return to the premodern situation where choice is squeezed out of the group. That would simply exchange an authoritarian, homogeneous state for an authoritarian, homogeneous church. It is the route of the cult. The way Paul allows for difference while holding the group together can be seen in Romans 14.

Paul sorts out an ethical mess

The background to the disagreement Paul handles in Romans 14 was cultural and individual. Jewish Christians were following Jewish practices prescribed by the Old Testament. They kept holy days, food laws and the like. Why should they cease to be Jews on becoming Christians? Gentile Christians, however, saw no need to observe such regulations. Why should they become Jews as well as Christians? Inside both communities, individuals were choosing differently. Suspicions were developing. For instance, before meat was sold in the market in Rome, the animal was often offered to a local deity. The Jewish conscience had a problem with eating the meat after that. Gentiles had eaten it all their lives without any ill effect. Now, Jewish and Gentile Christians were being asked to worship in the same church and eat at the same table. What does Paul say?

no legalism

First, he does not go down the legalist route. Paul had been a Pharisee, and legalism would have been a natural reaction for him. The Pharisees hedged the law of God around with hundreds of other rules for specific circumstances to keep God's people from breaking the law. Yet Paul refuses to make a ruling. He does not strictly apply the Old Testament law or make a new law. He gives his own opinion: 'I am fully convinced that no food is unclean in itself' (verse 14). But we have to decide for ourselves: 'Each one should be fully convinced in his own mind' (verse 5).

In his letter to the Galatians, Paul tells us that, as Christians, we have been freed from the law. What then is the nature of Christian freedom?

A confirmed bachelor who lived alone found it inconvenient to cook his own meals and wash his own shirts, so he hired a housekeeper. She cooked the curry just as he liked it. She ironed his shirts well. At the end of each week the man gave her the wages she was owed. Of course, if she had stopped doing the jobs, he would have had no alternative but to sack her and get someone else. But as time went on, they fell in love and got married. Suddenly the situation changed. Instead of wages at the end of the week, everything he had was hers. Instead of the possibility of the sack, there was complete security. But (being an old-fashioned girl) she still cooked his curry just the way he liked it. Why? She was no longer bound by a contract; there was no fear of dismissal for failure to cook it that way. But what he required of her when she was under law, she took as an indication of what pleased him. And so she continued to do those same things in a relationship of love.

That is how Christians look at the moral laws of the Old Testament.

the individual conscience

The second point Paul makes in Romans 14 is that we are each personally responsible before God for our choice. The ultimate motive is to please God. If we choose to eat the 'unclean' meat, we do it for him. If we choose not to eat it, we do it for him. 'If we live, we live to the Lord; and if we die, we die to the Lord' (verse 8). That means we should not judge another Christian who chooses differently from us. That person made his or her choice for God. God will make the judgment, and if we judge, we are usurping the role of God. 'Who are you to judge someone else's servant?' (verse 4). Very well, says Paul, we are to accept one another without reserve, even though we disagree. 'Accept him whose faith is weak, without passing judgment on disputable matters' (verse 1); 'Accept one another, then, just as Christ accepted you' (15:7).

But we are to go beyond mere acceptance: we are to love. And sometimes the most loving thing is to curtail our own freedom so that it does not harm the other person. There has been much misunderstanding about what Paul is saying here. His argument is based on the importance of conscience. As we have already implied, conscience is a useful guide to what is right and wrong, but is itself culturally conditioned. The consciences of Christians from different backgrounds can say different things about the same issue. Yet we must follow our conscience. 'If anyone regards something as unclean, then for him it is unclean' (verse 14). How so? If he believes that he will displease God by eating, then to eat is a sin. The same is true for any action we believe to be wrong, whether it is actually wrong or not. We must work to conform our conscience ever more closely to the will of God, but, in the meantime, we must obey it.

To push a fellow Christian into a position where he disobeys his conscience is to cause him to stumble (verses 13, 20). Paul does not mean that the weaker believer, on seeing the stronger eat the meat, will think it acceptable to do so, and thus eat and sin. Rather, he means that the weaker Christian will eat with the stronger for the sake of friendship or social imperative, and so go against his conscience and sin. If Paul had been writing for modern western Christians, he might have made the same point with regard to certain disputed forms of worship, drinking alcohol or the way people dress when they come to church.

the Christian and the world

Worldliness has always been an issue for Christians, but they have rarely agreed on what it means. 'The world', when the Bible speaks about it, can mean a variety of things. It is used of the whole universe; the word is literally 'cosmos' (Greek, *kosmos*). It is also used of the whole world of men and women, as in the statement that 'God so loved the world that he gave his one and only Son'. More particularly, it is used for the prevailing society or culture in so far as it is opposed to or different from the kingdom of God.[10] But we cannot entirely equate the world in this sense, the world we are to shun, with our present society or culture. Christians usually adopt one of three basic positions towards their society.

uncritical rejection

First, some reject 'the world' entirely. We see elements of this in some of the early Fathers, such as Tertullian, and later in Anabaptist and pietist groups. This decision finds its classic historical expression in monasticism. The standard evangelical response to this attitude is that the Bible tells us not to remove ourselves from the world; we are to be in it but not of it (Jn. 17:15–18). But this, like most clichés, conceals truth as well as revealing it. Some Old Testament prophets, as well as John the Baptist, Jesus and Paul, withdrew to the desert for a time. Jesus and Paul, while commending marriage, speak respectfully of those who opt out of this normal social arrangement. Periods of withdrawal from the world, decisions about lifelong celibacy, denying oneself for the sake of prayer: these are all to be found in the Bible.

The Protestant reaction against monasticism was strong. Some portrayed monks and nuns in sinister terms (as happened in England at the time of the dissolution of the monasteries under Henry VIII). But, despite much that was wrong with the system, there have been great saints in the monasteries and convents, people with a single purpose to live for God.

The world-denying attitude has often arisen as a counter to worldliness and compromise in the church. The growth of the monastic movement was given impetus by the conversion of Constantine, the first Christian emperor. The church then became respectable, and, as people flooded int it to gain political and social advantage, it also grew worldly. Many o those who believed that Christians should live a life of unworldly self sacrifice joined the monasteries and convents. Church historian Stephe Neill believes that the missionary societies enjoyed a similar function fo dedicated evangelicals in Victorian Britain. Luther and Calvin were right however, in rejecting the idea that those who left society achieved higher level of morality or spirituality. The highest Christian life can b lived in the bustle of the world.

Another expression of the world-rejecting attitude is the more recen evangelical concept of the world as enemy territory to be avoided. Thi stance, which evolved out of the pietism and premillennialism of the las century, allows Christians to enter the world for employment and othe necessary activity, but gives the impression that we must run back int the relative safety of a Christian environment as soon as possible. In orde to avoid the world as much as possible, we create sanitized versions of it activities so that Christians can enjoy them safely: Christian software slimming programmes, novels, rock concerts, films, schools, businesses and so on. Alternativism, however, generally produces but pale copies Non-Christian writers and artists often wrestle with issues in a deeper an less inhibited way than Christians. Where are today's serious 'Christian novels of adequate depth and power?

Ultimately, we cannot reject human society or human culture, becaus it is a part of us. To be human is to be cultural. Human beings do not jus express their own individuality; they are part of their society's expressio of its culture. Human culture is exciting and fascinating. Music and art literature and plays, films and debate are morally neutral vehicles for val ues which can be good or bad. To the extent that they express or occasio non-Christian values, they are worldly. Sometimes they convey values an knowledge which are uplifting, good and even Christian. Paul seems t endorse this attitude to his local culture when he tells the Philippia Christians to think about 'whatever is true, whatever is noble, whateve is right, whatever is pure, whatever is lovely, whatever is admirable' (Phil 4:8). Paul quoted Greek poetry to his Athenian audience (Acts 17:28) But nothing in this area is easy. Usually, good and evil values are mixe up in the same book or the same film.

uncritical acceptance

A second way of responding to our culture is with uncritical acceptance This view emphasizes God's activity outside as well as inside the church 'he neutrality, if not the inherent goodness, of the world is assumed in ›me expressions of Christian youth culture. In a number of countries, 'hristianity has adopted the political, racial and moral attitudes of the ate.

But culture is not always neutral or good. Because it is put together by nful men and women, it is very often the vehicle for evil values. This ultural or corporate sinfulness is the 'world' that Christians must oppose. Ve are told not to conform to the pattern of this world, but to be trans- ›rmed by the renewing of our minds (Rom. 12:2). Our criteria for choice re different because they are located in Christ and the Bible, and they equently come into conflict with those of the world.

Furthermore, the Bible tells us not only not to conform, but also not › love the world (1 Jn. 2:15). I take this to mean that even the good and 'holesome things in this world must be placed in a list of priorities. For xample, football is not wrong; sometimes it is neutral, sometimes it has ositive effects. But it is easy for some of us to rank it too highly in our ves. In particular, all the things of this world are contingent; they are assing away because they belong to the old order. Christians are already itizens of the new order and our love belongs there, seeking first God's ingdom, setting our hearts on things above (Mt. 6:33; Col. 3:1). When 'e get our priorities right, we find that the various ways in which we par- icipate in our culture become simultaneously less important and more njoyable.

areful critique

. third approach to culture is neither to accept nor to reject any of its xpressions without careful critical examination. We should evaluate ıeir contents, underlying values and results, and compare them with the ible's teaching on the issues involved. Some artistic or cultural expres- ons are unsuitable for Christians. Sometimes, despite negative preju- ice, they are entirely suitable and beneficial. Paul Hiebert gives an xample concerning hard rock music. Young people in an inner-city hurch in Los Angeles, mostly new converts from the gang and drug :ene, needed to work out a coherent Christian attitude to hard rock. The arents were against it and sought to prevent them listening at all. The outh pastor invited the young people to bring their hard-rock records to Bible study where he laid down some Christian guidelines. Then they layed each record one by one, evaluated it, and either retained or nashed it, depending on their decision.[11]

Sometimes the decision is less simple. A film or book may be a mixture of good and bad, and we have to make a judgment about the balance of its usefulness. An important factor here is self-knowledge: understanding how and why we as individuals react to the various elements. Another factor is how the judgment would fit into the collective decision-making of the believers in the area (though caution should be exercised if the group's inclination is oppressively negative towards the surrounding culture).

The two great biblical motifs of creation and redemption are relevant to this matter. If our understanding of the world were to be centred on redemption, we should see the world as essentially bad, in need of being redeemed. We should look to heaven as the ideal. The motif of creation is an essential balance. It sees the world as created and pronounced good by God. It looks not just to heaven but to a new heaven and a new earth. As Gerard Manley Hopkins wrote, 'The world is charged with the grandeur of God.' So is Tchaikovsky's Fourth Symphony. We need a theological balance: we should not reject this world that God has created and the beautiful things which he has enabled human beings to make; and neither should we accept this world uncritically, for it is a poor, sinful thing, in need of the redemption that is coming.

humanness and pleasure

Our humanness – that which belongs to human beings as human beings; that which was in the garden before sin and is in the world today despite sin; our nature as God's creation in his image – is something to believe in and delight in. To walk in the park and enjoy the sun and the trees, to shed a tear listening to a Chopin nocturne, to be moved by a play about love, to be excited about a game of football, to enjoy companionship and good food, sparkling eyes and physical beauty – such things, in the words of the psalmist, gladden the heart of man (Ps. 104:15), and are simple matters of thanksgiving.

Pleasure is related to our humanness. Joy in the Lord and what he has done for us is the constant right of all Christians. Pleasure is something we obtain from this world occasionally because we are human. Adam and Eve lived a life of pure pleasure. It was God's intention. As C. S. Lewis's Screwtape says about God, 'He's a hedonist at heart … he makes no secret of it, at his right hand are pleasures for evermore.' Ecclesiastes recommends the enjoyment of life. Calvin affirms that not to use for pleasure those created realities which are designed for our pleasure is to show ingratitude to the Creator.[12]

One such gift is the sexual relationship of husband and wife. The world has always been suspicious about Christians and sex. It is apt to charge that we not only believe sex outside marriage to be wrong, but that we believe sex itself to be sinful, or at least that its enjoyment is not very proper. This suspicion is well founded, for some Christians from Augustine onwards have indeed held that view. Augustine believed that the original sin in the garden was sex motivated by desire rather than by the command to procreate. It was the English Puritans (despite the connotations of that word today) who broke the mould, returned to the Bible, and understood marriage in terms of personal love and the enjoyment of each other.

the pressure to conform

We should never underestimate the power of the world to induce us to conform. It has always marketed its values and attitudes effectively. In any society, the rewards for conformity are great, and the penalties for being different hard to bear. The power of today's media in spreading the world's values, however, exceeds anything in history. The television especially, in advertisements, films and entertainment shows, subtly teaches a seemingly universal set of values about material things, power, pleasure, sex and security, which are not Christian.

As Christians we know ourselves to be different from the world. But as society pushes us into a corner and asks us to define that difference, we usually take our stand on the little, unimportant issues rather than the big ones. Jim Wallis tells of a time when he was dating a girl from a Christian family. He invited her to go with him to see *The Sound of Music*. But when he arrived at the house to collect her, he met her father in the doorway, barring the way. Father and daughter ended up in tears, and Wallis did not get to see the film with the girl. Later, he asked her father why he had vetoed the date. He replied, 'If we start going to movies and dances and start drinking and smoking, there will be absolutely nothing that makes us different from the world.' The tragedy is that he was probably right.[13]

Perhaps the most distressing fact about the average Christian and the average church in the West is that the features of both are almost entirely predictable on sociological grounds. There is too close a similarity between Christians and the world. Take, for instance, a non-Christian couple on £30,000 a year who live next door to a Christian couple on a similar income. Despite their different values relating to material things, it may not be easy to tell which is the Christian home. The clues will be there, of course – a notice saying 'Christ is the head of this house', the absence of ashtrays – but as to materialism, no clear distinction.

material possessions

On what big issues must we stand firm? Where, in our society, do we draw lines? There are many points at which we should do so, including attitudes to power, sex, and people of a different race or class from our own. One issue which stands out, however, and embraces many more, is materialism. It is natural for people in today's western society to concentrate on the material things of life. As urbanization and modernization develop, it is increasingly difficult to define identity in terms of family, group and community membership. Therefore, as Helga Dittmar writes in a recent sociological study of material possessions, 'it appears that *who we are* has been defined more and more through *what we have* as individuals; material possessions have become symbols of personal and social identity'.[14]

Our society, then, has a special relationship to possessions. Not only do we define our identity and worth in terms of possessions and wealth, but society itself seems to define quality of life in relation to possessions. Standard-of-living indexes count washing-machines and VCRs, salaries and disposable incomes. The quality of our life as human beings is measured economically. The logic of this is that in order to be happier we must possess more. This suits society because we are now in a system where greed is necessary for economic survival. In recessions, people borrow less and consume less – which in turn exacerbates the recession. Once we feel confident again, we shall take out our credit cards and buy what we have managed without till now, and the economy will revive. This is important to any government because its re-election depends, more than any other factor, on the state of the economy.

We can gain a shrewd idea of a society by looking at its heroes. One typical hero of western culture is the poor boy who makes good, the 'rags to riches' fairytale. The heroes of the church, by contrast, are more like rich boys who achieve poverty. Francis of Assisi (born about 1182 in Italy) has been a great example to Christians in many cultures and situations because he refused to conform to the world. He embraced lepers, was a man of constant, earnest prayer and, above all, married himself to the 'gracious lady poverty'. One day, he met a poor man on the road. He was about to give him his coat when his companions stopped him. 'I believe the Great Almsgiver will charge me with theft', he replied, 'if I do not give what I have to one who needs it more.' Perhaps more than anything else, Francis was remembered for being happy.[15]

conclusions

It has become plain that ethical issues are not always simple, particularly today. No-one can prescribe four spiritual laws which can be applied in every situation and then up pops the answer. A number of guidelines can be laid down, however, and these will serve to summarize this chapter.

1. *We must refuse legalism.* It never was an option for Christians. Sometimes it is manipulative – the game of the powerful who frame rules for the powerless. Sometimes it is benevolent – church elders trying to help young people by laying down what they should and should not do. In each age it has stifled the moral sense by letting a few do the hard work for all. In this age of diversity it is simply an impossible programme. There would be too many rules.

2. *But the moral baby must not be thrown out with the legalistic bathwater.* The Bible gives universally relevant norms, or descriptions of what pleases God. Sometimes the situation we are facing is sufficiently similar to one in the Bible to enable us to transfer a clear prohibition or command. Sometimes we have to apply a more general principle to a new situation. Occasionally we have to balance more than one principle and choose which is the more important in the circumstances.

3. *We must remember that there is a local, cultural bias in all our ethical decisions.* It affects our labelling of particular practices as sinful or not, the relevance of different commands in different situations, and the relative importance we place on specific sins. Cultural bias even twists biblical evidence to suit our *status quo*. Christians will use the Word to judge the world, praying at the same time that the Word will judge them and their hermeneutical bias.

4. *Christians should always obey their conscience.* In disputable matters, even when we get it wrong, all genuine attempts to please God *do* please God. In this complicated world where difficult choices continually press in on us, it is good to know that it is easier to please God than to get it right, even though we want to do both.

5. *Every decision involves a duty to our brothers and sisters in the Lord.* When, in all honesty, they try to please God as best they can, yet come to a conclusion different from ours, we must accept them in the same way as Christ has accepted us. He embraced us long before we got anything right. And we must take care never to put fellow Christians in a position where they would be under pressure to go against their conscience.

6. *The hermeneutical community is the church.* We do not have to face every issue from scratch, or on our own. We belong to a community of faith

which, to a certain extent, decides together. The idea that every Christian is a lone ranger would be Enlightenment individualism gone mad. We have to remember, however, that churches and Christian groups create their own subcultures which also bias our reading and application of the Scriptures. Usually, the church is dominated by the attitudes of an older rather than a younger generation. But it is a repository of wisdom. If today's situation does not match New Testament times, it may well be closer to yesterday's problem. The Spirit will guide us as we reflect on how he has guided our mothers and fathers in the faith and how he is guiding other believers. This way, we do not merely tolerate each other's differences; we move towards consensus.

7. *Remember that in Christ there is forgiveness for sin and freedom from the guilt of the past.* Socrates held that it is impossible deliberately to choose what is wrong, and that all wrong action is due to mistaken or confused belief. We know that not to be true. For every occasion on which we honestly try to do what is right, but get it wrong, there are ten occasions when we know what is right yet we go ahead and sin. Repentance and confession restore us, whether alone, or together at the sacrament of the Lord's table. We go on into life again with a clean sheet, because of the grace of Christ.

4. theology

There is greater diversity today in Christian belief and theology than in any previous generation.

doctrinal diversity

For most of us, the overwhelming variety of beliefs within Christianity needs an explanation. If there is one God, one Christ and one Bible, why do we not all believe the same? This question is felt more keenly among Protestants than Roman Catholics, because a strong central authority has done the choosing for the latter on many issues. Since Vatican 2, however, the issue has become conspicuous among that church's theologians. One of today's key areas of theological debate in Catholic circles is pluralism in theology.

Protestants have long championed the doctrines of the 'perspicuity of Scripture' and the 'right of private judgment' – meaning that the message of Scripture is clear and that any believer has the ability and the right, with the help of the Holy Spirit, to decide for himself or herself what it means. In practice this has led to thousands of Protestant denominations, as we shall see in the closing chapter.

The question 'Why such diversity?' is particularly difficult for evangelicals. We take the Bible as authoritative and believe that the Spirit lives in us to guide and help our thoughts and lives. Yet evangelicals, probably more than any other group, exhibit a tremendous diversity in what they believe. They disagree in the areas of baptism, the second coming, the work of the Holy Spirit, church government, the doctrine of election, and many other issues.

The usual explanation is that this variety arises from diversity of interpretation of the Scriptures; we disagree on what certain passages mean. Or, where two passages seem to teach different things, one group regards passage *A* as 'plain' and passage *B* as 'difficult', using *A* to interpret *B*. The other group sees it as the other way round, and so different conclusions are drawn.

We are now beginning to understand that we must ask deeper questions. Why does one interpretation seem more plausible to me? Why do I prefer one passage to another? Why is my choice different from yours? Earlier, we introduced Peter Berger's idea that we all operate within a plausibility structure which conditions our assessment of what it is reasonable to believe. We never read the Bible with a blank mind, but always bring to it our assumptions and presuppositions. To put it another way, there are social and cultural roots to doctrinal diversity and disagreement.

This is not an easy concept to accept. Most of us have been brought up in a church environment where we have been taught a historic confession, or at least were handed down a large body of beliefs which, to us, are the only way to interpret the Scriptures. All deviation from these must, we think, be false. We are 'mono-theological' Christians. For us, the idea that Scripture could be interpreted in different ways is disturbing. Theological diversity is as hard to handle as social diversity. The evangelical Willowbank Report's assertion that 'No theology is culture-free' is hard to accept, but is borne out by the following case studies.

how to run the church

The different denominations are divided on which form of church structure or government is right and biblical. The Anglican Church has episcopacy, centring around bishops who have authority over churches in their own areas. Presbyterians have a number of elders and pastors in a district, with joint authority over the churches in that area. Baptists and Congregationalists believe each local church to be independent of all other churches, and that the congregation or membership, when they meet together, should decide the church's business. These are only three of the structures common today, although many contemporary structures combine elements of the three basic positions. Most pastors or ministers in each of the main types will have no difficulty in 'proving' that their system is the biblical one.[1]

Yet these forms are not static. In September 1541, John Calvin gave birth to presbyterian church government by drafting his Ecclesiastical Ordinances for Geneva. He had in mind the government of a late medieval city state. When John Knox brought the system into Scotland, it had to be adapted for the use of an entire country. As it has settled down within modern democratic societies, the power of the church meeting, and therefore of the ordinary member in presbyterianism, has grown in a way Calvin would never have conceived. When it was taken to Nigeria by Samuel Bill a century ago, it developed within the Qua Iboe churches into virtually an episcopal system, with the 'area pastor' acting in many ways like a bishop. Presbyterianism, it seems, is a lively animal, able to adapt itself to the local culture and to accommodate itself to the prevailing authority structures in society.

There are various church structures in the New Testament. Titus was in charge of all the churches in the island of Crete. Timothy was over the elders in Ephesus. In Philippi there were elders and deacons. Paul appointed elders in all the churches in Asia Minor. In Jerusalem, James the brother of Jesus had a special authority. In Corinth, when Paul's letters were written, they seemed to have no elders but were ministered to by those with charismatic gifts. It is fruitless to try to harmonize this variety. Some have suggested that these churches were snapshots of the New Testament church as it developed towards a common model. But which was the goal towards which they were moving? Is the position of Titus in Crete (an episcopal model) the intended end of the development, or is it a sort of missionary stop-gap, a temporary expedient until the local churches mature and take over their own affairs?

It is likely that there was some development. But different church structures were appropriate to specific local conditions. Jewish Christians seem to have organized themselves on the basis of the synagogue model. This principle seems also to have obtained as the church has passed through different ideas of authority in society. The popularity of the congregational model today owes much to our plausibility structure influenced by democracy.

baptism

Baptism gives rise to doctrinal division among evangelicals today. May it be administered to infants, or should it be restricted to those mature enough to believe for themselves? Most churches feel that full unity across this divide is impossible. I was struck by the way baptism was handled in Nigeria. I worked in a group of about a thousand churches which held to the baptism of believers only. Before the missionaries came, boys and girls in that area underwent a rite of passage at puberty, bringing them into a spiritual society which offered them spiritual protection. Afterwards there was feasting in the family compound. I observed that the church baptized virtually all its children at around the age of puberty, stressed their membership of the church and endorsed the feasting which followed. A cultural factor was clearly at work.

On returning to the UK, I wondered whether this was true also of our own practice. Is western culture 'interfering' with our doctrines of baptism? We live now in a culture where society and family take fewer decisions for us, and the emphasis is on personal choice. The old system in which society and the family took most of the choices is breaking down. Could this explain why, in the last hundred years, those who hold to adult baptism have become a much larger percentage of Christendom than ever before? Perhaps today's culture-generated plausibility structure shifts us towards personal choice in the matter of baptism, and therefore away from infant baptism which has allowed the state or the parents a share in that choice. This second case study is different from the first because only one view can be right. Either babies should be baptized or they should not. But the example helps to show the extent of the cultural or societal factors in our decision-making on matters of doctrine.

These two case studies throw up a bundle of questions. Is this process inevitable? Is it healthy? Is it to be resisted or encouraged? A more subtle question is: 'In what circumstances, and to what extent, does this process indicate health or sickness?' We can tackle these questions and the whole problem of the diversity of doctrines only by taking a brief look at the nature of theology.

what is theology?

Theology since the Enlightenment is not what it used to be. Broadly, the word (from Greek *theos*, 'God', and *logos*, 'word' or 'reason') refers to any talk or reasoning about God. The old view of theology as 'the queen of the sciences' sprang from the premodern, prescientific idea that theology was the source of knowledge *par excellence*.

With the coming of the Enlightenment, the intellectual ride became rougher for theology. Along with every other discipline, it had to fight to establish its conclusions by reason and the use of evidence. The scientific method was finally applied to the queen of the sciences and she lost her crown. Nevertheless, in orthodox circles, it was still generally believed that theology was all about making universal truth claims concerning God and the spiritual world, although some theologians since Schleiermacher have preferred to speak of theology as a description of religious experience instead.

Occasionally theology has been closely wedded to the scientific method. For instance, one theological school influential among evangelicals is the Princeton school of Charles Hodge and Benjamin Warfield. Hodge believed theology to be simply the application of the scientific method to the raw facts of the Bible. The theologian proposes hypotheses and tests them in an impartial way. But such an attitude will not do. The philosophers of science Michael Polanyi and Thomas Kuhn have shown that the scientific method is anything but impartial. We are involved in the construction of our world. To Hodge they would say, 'You are involved in the construction of your theology.' And this is evidently so.

Because both the theologian and his or her situation are involved in the construction of theology, it is important to distinguish between theology and the Word of God. Theology is human. The Word of God is divine revelation. This emphasis on the humanity of theology preserves a proper humility about our theological constructions, particularly when they differ from those of a fellow Christian.

Theology, then, is not something given (as the Word of God is). Theology is something we do. It is a task. One useful way to think of it is as a bridge between two points. One point is the Word of God. The other is the specific situation in which the theologian lives and ministers. The theologian's task is to build that bridge, to bring the Word of God into that situation. It follows that both the Bible and the situation influence the way theology is put together.

theology across cultures

How does the theologian undertake this task upon moving to a new cultural setting?

Over the last thirty years many missionary lecturers have been trained in the West and sent to the Third World to 'teach' the growing church. Most shared the older idea of theology as a set of theorems about God (and related subjects) which enshrine unchangeable, supracultural, objective truth. Accordingly, they took their notes, given to them by their own teachers, and delivered the material to their African, Asian or South American students. It did not work well. I know because I did it and have talked with others who fell into the same trap. But what was wrong with that method? Two newer sciences are of help here.

Anthropology has shown us that there are as many different cultures as there are peoples in this world. If cultures are really packages of values, beliefs and worldviews in specific geographical and historical locations, theology is the expressing of the truths of God in terms understood within each of those packages. It need not be western to be valid. As theology is done in different cultures, we end up with different theologies which are none the less united as expressions, in their contexts, of the same Word of God.

Parallel to this growing awareness of cultures, communication science was progressing. This was developed as a theory of translation by scholars such as Eugene Nida and adapted for theology by Charles Kraft[2] and others. It emphasizes the hearer as the star. True communication takes place only when the hearer receives fundamentally the same thought that the communicator wants to convey. In a missionary situation, three cultures are involved. The teacher must understand the biblical culture so that the truth can be extracted; he must recognize that his own western cultural clothes, to an extent, distort his own theology; and he must deeply understand the hearer's culture so that the truth can be presented without distortion as it passes through the hearer's cultural grid. A daunting task.

The process can be illustrated from a hymn by John Newton.

> Jesus! my Shepherd, Saviour, Friend,
> My Prophet, Priest and King,
> My Lord, my Life, my Way, my End,
> Accept the praise I bring.

Each of these pictures of Jesus is understood differently in different cultures. Shepherds in Palestine go before the sheep. Shepherds in Britain do not need to drive away wolves. Shepherds in West Africa go behind the flock with a big stick. Priests in Jewish culture had a different function from priests in post-Reformation Protestant Europe, and the word had a different emotional resonance; their significance is different again in Thailand and in France. Kings in the Old Testament are very different from monarchs in Europe, and different again from chiefs in Africa. Even the picture of Christ as our End assumes a linear concept of time that is alien to many in India.

In fact, every picture of Christ has a positive and negative content. The writer of the book of Hebrews realized this when he described Christ as the great high priest. He felt it necessary to say that Christ is like the high priest of Judaism in some ways, but not in others (for instance, he had no need to offer sacrifices for his own sins). As a picture crosses a cultural boundary, the balance of its positive and negative content shifts, and it becomes either more useful in that culture or less so. For instance, the biblical picture of Christ as our elder brother was useful in New Testament times because the elder brother had an important socially defined role in that culture. That is not true of western culture in our own day, so the analogy has been used less by Christians here. Every part of Scripture is needed to give a balanced picture of Christ.

Inadequacies of cross-cultural communication have impacted mission in practical ways. In many parts of Africa, one can drive for hours through the bush and then suddenly come across a clearing with a magnificent church building in the centre. Westerners would often recognize it as a carbon copy of the buildings they worshipped in back home. Inside, they realize that such buildings in the West were designed to keep the heat in, whereas what is needed in Africa is more ventilation.

Historically, missionaries have taken the view that the simplest way to plant a church, once there was a group of converts, was to use their own home church as a model. Accordingly, Baptist, Anglican, Presbyterian, Methodist and a hundred other western denominations are scattered across the Third World. We have exported not just our architecture, but also our own unfortunate western divisions because of a misunderstanding about how to do theology. Just when they could have started afresh, we have passed on to them our own ambiguous history.

But this is changing. Many missionary candidates nowadays are taught to plant indigenous churches, taking the fundamental truths about the church from the New Testament and marrying them to what is good in the host culture, under the guidance of the Holy Spirit. But they have an unenviable task writing back to their supporters in, for example, Scottish Presbyterian churches explaining why they are not planting Scottish Presbyterian churches in Ivory Coast.[3]

Even language is not neutral. At a prayer meeting in southern Nigeria, one is quite likely to hear the old men begin their prayers with 'O Jehovah' and the young men with 'O Abasi'. How did such a situation come about? When the missionaries first came to southern Nigeria, they found a word in the Efik language, 'Abasi', which was used for the one high god. Abasi was in some ways like the God of the Bible: he was creator and judge. But he was not loving or close to men and women. So the early missionaries decided not to use that name, but to import a word instead: Jehovah, the Authorized Version's translation of the Hebrew name of the God of the Old Testament. Later, younger missionaries and Nigerians objected to this as a sign of western pride. They reverted to the local word Abasi, but changed its content by their preaching and teaching. This is not the place to say who was right, but the example demonstrates the need to think deeply even about the word we use for 'God' if we are to transmit the gospel faithfully.

The thesis of Kosuke Koyama's book *Three Mile an Hour God* (1979) is simple. The western view of time has been imposed upon our view of God. We expect him to be in a hurry. The fast-food culture expects instant solutions from God. We are dominated by the speed of the car – fifty miles an hour or more. But God's working is much closer to the walking pace of three miles an hour. He spent forty years teaching Israel one lesson in the desert: that human beings do not live by bread alone.

Koyama says 'God walks "slowly" because he is love ... Love has its speed, it is a different kind of speed from the technological speed to which we are accustomed.'[4] Theology is as diverse as the experiences of people in every culture of the world.

the lessons of history

We do not have to cross the world to see how the situation and the theologian contribute to theology. The history of theology has been the story of the way the Word of God has been expressed in different situations, cultures and philosophies at different stages of history.

Each historical period, as well as each geographical place, comes with an integrating package of philosophy and attitudes: in other words, a culture. While this package is accepted without question by almost everyone in its own time and place, when we look back on it from a different time and a different package we see its omissions and errors. Almost no-one in the thousand years of the Middle Ages questioned that the Sun moved round the Earth, the right of the pope to depose kings, the burning of books and the execution of heretics. It was all part of the package. The challenge facing Christians in every era is to avoid blindly accepting the thought-forms of the day, but rather to discern them and, as far as it can be done faithfully, express the truth in those forms.

We can see this happening within the Bible itself. James Dunn's book *Unity and Diversity in the New Testament* (1977) caused a stir by questioning whether there was one homogeneous orthodoxy in early Christianity. Did the situation and the individuality of each leader make that impossible? He found a variety of theological positions within the New Testament on the person of Christ, ministry, worship, early preaching and other matters. He concluded that this diversity in unity points the way for today's church.[5]

Dunn went too far in regarding these various theological formulations as incompatible. He did demonstrate that there is diversity in New Testament theology, but he failed to show that it arose from the different situations in which theology was being done. The gospel crossed a cultural barrier within the New Testament. Christianity began as a Jewish movement and quickly entered the Greek-dominated Gentile world.

Much contextual theology was done over that divide by Paul. He searched for language and concepts from the new culture which could be pressed into service. Instead of presenting Jesus as the Christ (the Jewish term for 'messiah'), he preferred the term 'Lord', which signified 'God' in the Greek translation of the Scriptures, and the 'emperor' in popular usage. He took the word 'reconcile' as a picture of the work of Christ. He called the missionary giving of the Philippian church a 'libation', which was a form of pagan sacrifice involving pouring out wine or water. Some scholars think that in writing to the Colossians, he even borrowed words from the heresy he was attacking and brought them into the service of the truth. For instance, he used the word *plērōma*, which we translate 'fullness', to describe the divine perfection of Christ. It would have been recognized by his first readers as the term for the many intermediaries between God and humanity in the heretics' religious system. Paul created Greek Christian theology.

After the New Testament period, a number of heresies arose as Christians tried to understand how Jesus could be both God and human. A council was convened at Chalcedon in 451 to settle the matter. It defined the person of Christ in the philosophical language of the time, strongly influenced by Plato, Aristotle and their disciples. In particular, it said that Christ, though one person, had two natures, human and divine. These were defined in static terms, as two substances which were not mixed but existed side by side in Christ. Out of that view came the idea that by means of his incarnation, taking human flesh, the second person of the Trinity could manifest himself in both natures.

Chalcedon defended the humanity and divinity of Christ in the philosophical terms and thought-forms of the day. Nowadays, we think of human nature and persons in a different way, so in the last thirty years there has been a reaction against the language of Chalcedon, led by theologians who prefer 'dynamic' Christologies to the old, static, 'substance' terminology. More recent philosophies such as existentialism, and now the process philosophy of Alfred North Whitehead and Charles Hartshorne, speak of our developing into persons by our interaction with our environment and with other persons, and by the choices we make. We are becoming, rather than being. Process theologians argue that we should understand the personhood of Christ in the same way.

It is unfortunate that many dynamic Christologies are unable to fit some of the fundamental truths about Christ (such as his pre-existence or his place in the Trinity) into their system. They thus become heretical and must be rejected by the faithful. Nevertheless, although their answers are often wrong, we have to face the questions they faced. Does theology have to be tied down to a philosophy of 1,500 years ago? Is that the only terminology for talking about Christ? Or should we follow the lead of the bishops at Chalcedon by defending the full deity and humanity of Christ in the language and philosophy of today?[6]

Christians have often preferred to hold on to the past rather than fight the battles of the day. They usually do so by appealing to their historic confessions. The Anglican Church has the Thirty-nine Articles. The Presbyterian churches have the 'subordinate standards' (Scripture is the primary standard) of the Westminster Confession and the Longer and Shorter Catechisms. Other denominations have similar historic confessions. There is a great advantage in these statements of faith. They preserve continuity and give a sense of identity, even though they have not proved to be the bulwark against heresy many would wish them to be.

These confessions, however, are clearly not enough. The task of theology is not done when the statements are repeated and explained. As we have seen, the concerns of one culture and generation are not those of another. The heresies and sins of one society differ from those of another. Because each age has its blinkers, it cannot lay down a standard for all ages. It is impossible for the theology produced in England in the sixteenth and seventeenth centuries to be adequate for Africans (or even the English) on the verge of the twenty-first. For instance, none of them makes more than a negligible reference to the task of world mission or the issue of social responsibility. They were a product of an age which, for a variety of reasons and amid a number of other pressing concerns, did not adequately come to terms with the missionary task or the churches' social engagement with the world.

academic theology today

How then do academic theologians take account of such thinking? In 1988, seventy theologians, sociologists of religion and philosophers came together for a conference in the German town of Tübingen. Most of the big names in academic theology were there, both Catholic and Protestant. They came to discuss how far the insights of Thomas Kuhn, in particular (see chapter 1), relate to theology. They proved that what George Bernard Shaw is reported to have said about economists is true also of theologians – that if all of them were laid end to end, they would not reach a conclusion. They did, however, agree on some points, and one was that we cannot go back to the old view of theology as an objective science. We must recognize that theology is bipolar, and that the situation in which it is done affects the task; indeed, it *should* do so. David Tracy, in summarizing the findings of the conference, said that 'In spite of a wide and growing plurality of particular models for theology, there does seem to be a shared general model for theological reflection in our period.' He went on to define this agreement as including the view that 'theology [is] hermeneutical ... an attempt to develop mutually critical correlations in theory and practice between an interpretation of the Christian tradition and an interpretation of the contemporary situation'.[7]

This basic view of theology as operating out of two poles – Christian sources and the situation in which the theology is done – is shared by most evangelical theologians. David Wells, a prominent North American evangelical theologian, defines the task of theology as 'to discover what God has said in and through Scripture and to clothe that in a conceptuality which is native to our own age. Scripture, as its *terminus a quo*, needs to be de-contextualised in order to grasp its transcultural content, and it needs to be re-contextualised in order that its content may be meshed with the cognitive assumptions and social patterns of our time.'[8]

Academic theology today, whether evangelical or decidedly non-evangelical, generally recognizes the dual polarity of theology. But evangelicals and non-evangelicals view the two poles differently. Evangelical theologians will ensure that it is the pole of the Word of God which is normative or determinative for theology's content and emphasis, as Wells indicates.

the postmodern theology of David Tracy

One non-evangelical theologian who has perhaps done more in this area than any other is David Tracy, Professor of Theology at Chicago Divinity School. Tracy has concerned himself especially with pluralism and diversity in theology and has written two major books on the subject, *Blessed Rage for Order* and *The Analogical Imagination.*[9]

He begins by rejecting the traditional view of theology. What has been seen as plain truth in theology, he says, is really historically and culturally conditioned tradition. People cannot slough off their cultural skin; no interpreter of the Bible is entirely impartial. We must turn therefore to the newer hermeneutical models of Hans-Georg Gadamer, Paul Ricoeur and to a lesser extent Jürgen Habermas (see chapter 1). These (as we have seen) envisage two poles or horizons: the horizon of the classical text (for the Christian, the Scriptures), and the horizon of our present situation, out of which and in which we read the text. A conversation is created between these -- a true hermeneutical circle in which each pole modifies the other. Truth comes in a correlation of the two. Tracy calls this view of theology the 'revised correlationist paradigm'.

Much that Tracy says can be applauded. His construction reinforces the humanity, even the sinfulness, of theologians and theologies with their cultural content. He does not, however, seem to give enough place to the final authority of Scripture in the process, because he insists that *both* horizons must move. For Tracy, there has to be mutual transformation, mutual correlation. But because Scripture is the inspired, revealed Word of God, it must be *the* authority, *the* source of truth. There are not two sources of truth, however, but one, even though there may be two sources for our human constructions of theology. One pole must control the other. Only one pole can move. It is the task of Scripture to modify our understanding, even our questions.

Tracy might object that we can never get to truth itself, and that we can work only with our interpretations and our Christian interpretive traditions. But this denies the Christian doctrines of inspiration and illumination. Given that God has decisively revealed himself in Jesus Christ, he will surely make possible the accurate communication of that revelation. There is such a thing as epistemological grace, the Holy Spirit's supervision of the writing of the Bible and his work in interpretation.

political theology

To what extent can we allow politics to influence the human pole of theology, and so play a part in generating theological diversity? Politics and religion are fundamental to the human condition, and it is hard to separate them. The frequently repeated plea to keep politics out of religion almost always falls on deaf ears. Through the ages they have fed off each other, and naturally so. Politics is one area of culture, and it is impossible to form a theology concerned with what is going on in society without getting involved in politics (Greek *polis* = Latin *societas*). Is it likely that God would be interested in everything pertaining to human beings except politics, even though politics makes such a difference to their happiness or misery? There must surely be political as well as private applications of the gospel.

There are a number of expressions of political theology, but this section concentrates on the best-known, liberation theology – bearing in mind that this is a large and diverse movement containing some elements which rightly challenge us and some which cannot be accepted as truly biblical theology.

On 9 May 1985, in Brazil, a Franciscan theologian named Leonardo Boff received a letter from Cardinal Ratzinger in Rome ordering him not to preach, write or give interviews. It was an important shot across the bows of liberation theology. It backfired, however, because all it served to lo was to bring the movement to the attention of the world.

Liberation theology is another 'two pole' theology, as the first sentence of ts best-known book, *A Theology of Liberation* by Gustavo Gutiérrez, makes lear: 'This book is an attempt at reflection, based on the Gospel and the xperience of men and women committed to the process of liberation.'[10] In ther words, it considers both the gospel and the task of liberation together. Ie states later that it is 'a new way to do theology'.

But it is similar to postmodern theologies in several ways. To begin vith, it rejects the traditional attitude to theology stemming from the nlightenment. It does not regard itself as a disinterested, impartial sci-nce, isolated from the current of humanity. It does not operate out of the iniversities or strive for independence from the social situation or the noment in history. Instead, liberation theology opts for a particular ermeneutical circle. For Juan Luís Segundo, this begins by accepting the ocial situation. It then comes to the gospel or the text of Scripture with uestions derived from that situation (and especially with a suspicion that ast interpretations and applications have been done on behalf of the *sta-us quo*). The interaction with the text causes the liberation theologian to o back to social reality and change it, which then starts the process all ver again.[11]

ocialism and Christ

The theology of liberation is concerned with a particular type of politics: hat of the Left or, as its exponents would prefer to put it, that of the poor nd powerless masses. In Latin America the church has always got nvolved in politics, but usually it has bolstered oppressive regimes, be-tified capitalism and been on the side of the rich. This has been a general attern across the world, with theologians in Rome, Manchester and Princeton, as well as Lima, São Paulo and Mexico City, refusing to criticize he system which gives them secure jobs in universities and comfortable ars while much of the world starves. Is it not the duty of theologians also o love? In 1968, the general conference of the Latin American episcopacy net in Medellín in Columbia, and declared that God opts for the poor, and o must the church.

Such theologians have frequently used Marxist theory in the construc-ion of their theology. And why should they not choose to do so? Other reas of the church use capitalist presuppositions – such as equating the ystem of capitalist enterprise with freedom, and emphasizing private ather than public possessions. What these men and women are saying is hat it is not enough to try to contextualize the gospel into (say) Brazil as a whole, because its society is so diverse. Rather, they look for the cor cerns of Christ in Brazil and find that these rest primarily with the ma ginalized and the poor. They wish to contextualize theology for the particularly.

They say that one way in which traditional theology has failed the poo of Latin America is in concentrating almost exclusively on three aspec of salvation: that it is personal, not corporate; spiritual, not material; an for the hereafter, not the present. This offer of 'pie in the sky when yo die' by the church has made the oppression of the poor easy. It h involved interpreting the Bible in a specific way. For instance, tradition theologians spiritualize many Old Testament passages, including one th is central to liberation theology, the story of the exodus from Egypt. Th event has been taken out of context and used by western Christians as n more than a prefiguring of personal spiritual salvation. First of all, the logians of liberation argue, it should be allowed to speak of God's desi to lead his people out of oppression and poverty in this world.

Thus we return to the issue of action. For some liberation theologie this is fundamental. For them, it is not just that Christians should act i such situations, but that theology itself arises out of the act. Theology critical reflection on the struggle and the gospel; it is a theology of *praxi* of action. To see oppression and do nothing is to side with the oppresso Those who refuse to engage in praxis develop a theology to justify the inaction. To see oppression and to act is a precondition for good theolog good actions produce good theology.

But should this action ever be *violent*? Can Christians further the stru gle for liberation by using the gun in certain circumstances? Wester Christians have both abhorred and been fascinated by violence, bu mostly they have abhorred it. 'Gentle Jesus, meek and mild', a moder western picture of Jesus, does not take account of the fact that there w at least one violent act in his ministry – the cleansing of the temple wit a whip. Frantz Fanon envisages an initial act of liberating force: 'Violenc is a cleansing force; it frees the native from his inferiority complex an from his despair and inaction; it makes him fearless and restores his sel respect.'[12]

It is notable that it is force by the powerless and oppressed which usually labelled 'violence', not the actions of those already in power. Thi says Helder Camara, is unfair. A poor man may be punished for stealin to keep his family, but it may well be the accuser who is responsible fc his poverty. The poor man may hold up a passer-by with a gun, but a bi industrialist may hold a whole community to ransom. Is financial vi ence less culpable than that committed with a firearm?

What about violence as part of one's love for one's neighbour? Imagine hree men living in the same street: John, Jim, and Chris the Christian. One day John runs into Chris's house with a bleeding head because Jim nas hit him with a club. Chris, like the good Christian he, is binds up the wound and sends him back. The next day it happens again, and the next. What is Chris's duty? Why have we assumed that Christian love requires is only to bind up the wounds caused by others? Love surely demands hat we put an end to the wounding by confronting Jim and forcibly estraining him if necessary. And what if Jim is the government and John s the poor? The Christian church has often sanctioned force in defence of tself or its doctrine. Why not in defence of the poor?

It must be said, however, that by no means all liberation theologians nave gone down this route. Most advocate revolution without violence.

critique

Liberation theology teaches us much about the nature of faith in the conext of this evil world. It rightly tells us that we truly believe only if we act. It reminds us that theology is no ivory-tower pursuit, but an act of pecific love for a group of people performed by someone who is involved and who cares. God's love for the poor and Christ's saving of the prositute are more important subjects for right belief than the nature of the union between the divine and human in Christ and the correct form of church government.

Yet we must question a number of elements in liberation theology. Is Marxist theory the best tool for understanding society? More importantly, n its emphasis on social problems and freedom from oppression, liberaion theology does not pay enough attention to sin and salvation in the context of the individual's personal relationship with God. Fundamentally, its hermeneutical method, commencing as it does with praxis, seems o restrict God's Word to a secondary position, a basis for reflection after social action has taken place. This diminishes the authority of God's revelation and can produce unbalanced theology.[13]

laying down the rules

The fact that theology is constructed out of the Word of God and the situation or culture in which we are immersed follows the pattern of God's dealings with this world. In his incarnation, Christ, the Word of God, took not just flesh, but first-century Jewish flesh. He was circumcised and presented in the temple, and fully participated in the culture of his time and place. Paul echoed this when he said that he became a Jew to win the Jews. Theology must do the same. Like Christ (though in a much qualified sense), it is human and divine. It is this humanness of theology, as well as its divinity, which is responsible for so much of the variety we see today.

As we have also seen, however, this perception is often applied in such a way as to be inadequately Christian and to deny the Word of God. The great issue in theology today is the relationship between theology's divinity and humanity. Just as the early church had to work out the relationship between Christ's humanity and divinity, so we have to do a similar task today for theology. That task is by no means complete, and various solutions are being proposed at present. But we can lay down some ground-rules for the task.

God's revelation must be in control

From time immemorial, people have been doing to God's Word what Procrustes did to his overnight visitors. They have tried to stretch it or trim it to fit their culture and philosophy, instead of conforming these things to God's Word.

The two poles between which theology is constructed are not equal. The divine pole, God's Word, must judge the human, and not *vice versa*. The Word of God has always judged the cultures it has entered. It alone is the location of authority in theology. It says to society, 'This is wrong', 'This practice is evil', 'That belief is false.' It convicts the world of sin and error. God says no as well as yes. Of course, we must ensure that we allow the Word itself, and not our culture-bound reading of it, to make the judgment.

There are many ways of attempting to combine the Word of God with the situation which lead to false theologies. No theology can deny any truth that is found in the Word of God. The fourth-century heretic Arius applied Neoplatonism rigidly to Christ, concluding that since God was a unitary being, Christ must be a creature and not divine. Process theology, when it finds no place for the pre-existence of Christ, is a false theology. It too has failed to allow the divine pole to judge the human category as inadequate. As we have seen, David Tracy has not given due weight to the authority of the Word of God in the production of theology.

The fact is that no single worldview or human construction arising out of a specific situation can fully embrace the truth of the Word of God. All good theology, while being as contextual as possible, in the end has to be eclectic, borrowing from more than one source of ideas and concepts to express the truth fully. Theology must be like a building, some parts of which can be built with one type of framework, other parts requiring another. It is instructive that God's truth is expressed in the Bible within two different worldviews and thought patterns, the Hebrew and the Greek. Perhaps it was necessary.

balance

The Word of God must also judge the balance of any theology. Many theologies have gone wrong, not so much by denying a part of the Word as by overemphasizing one part to the detriment of others. This often happens when we allow the world and its problems to set the agenda for theology. Yet it is valid to emphasize particular aspects of truth in certain circumstances. In a situation of oppression and poverty, it is right to stress God's love for the poor. But in so doing we must not lose sight of the reality and importance of personal salvation.

Many evangelical church members will have heard the story of the judge who finds his own son in the dock before him on a charge. He is not lenient; he imposes the maximum fine. But who pays the fine? The judge steps down from the bench and, acting now as the boy's father, gets out his chequebook and pays it all himself. It is a good picture of how God deals with our sin by himself discharging the penalty imposed by his own law.

But many Christians do not realize that the idea of satisfying God's justice is only one of the pictures by which the Bible explains the work of Christ. In a society which understands and emphasizes the concept of law, such legal pictures are especially useful. In a society where slavery is part of the social structure, the picture of redemption from slavery is useful. In a society which practises sacrifice, we can highlight the picture of propitiation by the sacrifice of Christ. Each of these pictures on its own is inadequate to convey the full meaning of Christ's work. Whether we use the other pictures or not, therefore, we need to include in our explanations the truths they contain.

faithful communication

The fact that God has revealed himself in Jesus Christ as the Lord and Saviour of the world, and that the church is commanded to take that message to all peoples, implies that there is a body of supracultural norms which can be translated into every language and culture on earth. This task centres on the great themes of the gospel and requires repentance, a response of faith in Christ, conversion and the beginning of a church in a new place.

It can (indeed, sometimes must) be done by people from a different culture. It is initially a missionary task. Often in the last two centuries, although less often today, this missionary task has been performed by western Christians in the Third World. In such circumstances it involves decontextualization; missionaries must do all they can to strip the gospel of its western cultural baggage. They must then recontextualize it clothing the gospel in the language and thought-forms of the receptor culture. Some have been able to do this, but few have done the job well, or until recently, have seen the need to do either task.

The most appropriate model for this task is that of translation.[14] Charles Kraft and Eugene Nida make good use of this model, as we saw earlier in the chapter. It is not a matter of a simple, word-for-word correspondence, for that would not necessarily convey the same truth. We must translate the *meaning*, aiming for what Kraft calls the 'dynamic equivalence' – language that produces the same result in the new hearers as the original did in its hearers. Mere word-for-word equivalence is not sufficiently faithful to the original, because too much meaning is lost.

There is also the issue of relevance. The gospel is always relevant to every individual and people, but each individual and people must be helped to perceive that relevance. Preachers of the gospel in the West rightly emphasize the disorientation and purposelessness of life today without Christ. They speak of the sins of the times. Jesus is proclaimed as Lord over a so-called closed scientific universe and chance happenings. Preachers in Africa, by contrast, speak of Jesus as Lord over evil spirits and witchcraft; they denounce idolatry and corruption.

incarnation

The task of incarnating the gospel cannot be done entirely by the cross-cultural missionary, but is rather the task of the local Christians themselves. It involves much more than proclaiming the gospel; it means working out the relevance of every part of the Word of God for every part of the culture. The translation model is inadequate here, and we must make use of some sort of hermeneutical circle.[15]

This kind of 'incarnation' shows itself in surface issues such as church architecture, as we have already seen. It also shows itself in the architecture of authority in the church – its government. But it means more than merely clothing the Word in new garments; it means really taking flesh and dwelling among the people of this culture. Someone has well described it as planting the seed of the Word in a new soil and watching it grow. It is in one sense a 'theology from below' as the situation is allowed to ask its own questions of the Word of God, and not just study the questions westerners asked four centuries ago. The deep cultural needs and the complicated cultural situation of the West today must be brought face to face with the Word of God. Truth must be expressed, as far as possible, in contemporary philosophical categories and in modern words. And out of new questions will come truth which was hidden until it was unlocked by those specific questions.

This process enriches theology done in other parts of the world and other cultures too. Theological education can easily degenerate into a sterile picking over old bones. Deeper understanding arises from new perspectives. The Asian perspective will inform the western; the African will inform the South American.

conclusions

1. *The traditional idea of theology can no longer be supported.* It is not an academic task for a few intellectuals in a classroom. Theology is not a science. It is the task of the church. It is evangelism; it is mission. In the New Testament, it was not done in isolation from the proclamation of the gospel or the pastoral care of the saints. It was done by working missionaries and pastors. In a real sense, it is done by all Christians as they seek to relate the whole Bible to the world they live in.

2. *The very nature of theology requires lay involvement.* The church cannot talk about matters of life and death without inviting Christian doctors into the discussion, or about materialism when Christian economists are not present. If theology means relating the Word of God to the social and cultural situation, the whole church is needed to do the job. It is as concerned Christians ask questions of the Bible, and find in turn that their questions are modified by encountering the Word of God, that the task of theology is done.

3. *Our first obligation is to be faithful.* All who believe in God's self-revelation in the Scriptures desire first of all to be scrupulous in their proclamation of that revelation. A cafeteria-type theology, where we choose what we fancy as we move along, is not an option. We have to be faithful to the Word not only in its truth but also in its emphases.

4. *The packages of truths presented in our churches do not derive from the Bible alone.* They contain the Word of God in a framework of historical concerns, cultural emphases and other biases. That baggage is on our back as

we come to read the Bible, and affects the way we interpret it. We should therefore adopt a certain attitude of suspicion towards these packages. Many church groups will ask us to agree with them on detailed, disputable issues before offering us fellowship, but we cannot hand over our own critical faculties to a group in this way. Of course every church has a right to ask us to agree with them on the fundamental issues of the gospel, but they cannot ask us to side with all the cultural and situational interpretations of the Word of God which they also hold.

5. *We should not attach an exaggerated importance to the historic statements of faith.* The danger does not lie so much in signifying our assent to them (if we are happy with everything in them), but in thinking that they are enough. The task of applying the Bible to today still needs to be done.

6. *If we believe, we must act.* Theology is about love as well as truth. If it is true that people are lost without Christ, that judgment will come, that God is compassionate, that the church is the body of Christ, and that humankind was made for God, we must act out the implications. But we must be wary of beliefs which seem at first glance to come out of the Bible, but which in fact result in unchristian practice; any belief which props up the *status quo* (political or otherwise), produces oppression, or allows us to ignore the weak, the hurting and the poor. By their fruits we know them.

7. *We should not try to do theology alone, or even solely with Christians from our own tradition.* We need the perspective of Christians from different cultures, periods and movements in the church to balance and correct our own bias. Denominational loyalty has a price tag in theology. It is only 'together with all the saints' that we understand the love of God (Eph. 3:18). In times of pluralism in theology, we need more than ever the perspective of the one, worldwide church.

8. *We should take a generous view of Christians from the past.* Is ours the only age when Christians have not worn cultural blinkers? One day our blinkers will be as evident to the next generation as those of previous generations are to us. But did those earlier Christians love God fully and trust Christ only? Then we can forgive them as we hope to be forgiven.

9. *We must relate the unchangeable story of Christ and his salvation to our contemporaries in the words, thought-forms and vehicles appropriate to their culture and situation.* This applies whether we are speaking of Christ in Uganda, among inner-city youngsters in London or among students with a postmodern attitude to life and truth. As we speak, we must point out the inadequacies of the vehicle we are using. But there is no other vehicle.

5. mission

The church, if it does not reach out to the world, ceases to reflect not only its own character but the very character of God. As we consider the ways in which the church reaches out today, once again we find an amazing diversity.

diversity in mission

The church's mission today is diverse in both its content and its method. We shall look at each in turn.

There are now so many ways of getting involved in mission. Would-be missionaries can offer themselves as church-planters, Bible teachers, secretaries, children's workers, agriculturalists, managers, accountants, pilots, radio engineers, drivers, pharmacists, printers, nurses, doctors, teachers, linguists, shipping agents, and much more. In fact, there is hardly a profession or skill which is not seen as relevant to the missionary task today.

This has not always been the case. When the modern missionary movement commenced on the back of the growing British Empire, missionaries had a fairly standard job description. They had to be pioneer evangelists and church-planters in the style of C. T. Studd or the young Hudson Taylor. This quickly changed. Missionaries soon brought with them western institutions which required, at least initially, western personnel to run them. Schools needed teachers; hospitals needed nurses and doctors. Later, as both the work and the world became more complicated, an ever wider range of skills was required.

a wider definition

Another reason for this diversity of personnel is that the definition of mission itself has significantly broadened in the twentieth century. It was the Jerusalem conference of the International Missionary Council in 1928 that first talked of the 'comprehensive approach' to mission. A move was afoot to encourage the church to engage with the world in all its needs and hopes, rather than solely with individuals and their spiritual salvation.[1]

This shift was quickly followed among evangelicals. The traditional evangelical view had been that involvement with the other, 'non-spiritual' needs of individuals and the world was simply a matter of showing Christian compassion rather than a part of the missionary task. Action to relieve human distress, whether in medical work or famine relief in the Third World, or in city-mission work at home, was usually initiated in order to create an opportunity for preaching the gospel. But Carl F. H. Henry, a prominent evangelical thinker, wrote in 1947: 'Fundamentalism in revolting against the Social Gospel seemed also to revolt against the Christian social imperative ... It does not challenge the injustices of the totalitarians, the secularisms of modern education, the evils of racial hatred, the wrongs of current labor–management relations, and inadequate bases of international dealings.'[2]

This change of heart rapidly gained popularity, culminating in the Lausanne Congress in 1974, which incorporated social action into the mission of the church. Afterwards, the chief architect of the Lausanne Covenant, John Stott, explained that he had changed his mind. Having previously interpreted the missionary task of the church in exclusively evangelistic terms, now, he wrote, 'I see more clearly that not only the consequences of the commission, but the actual commission itself, must be understood to include social as well as evangelistic responsibility, unless we are to be guilty of distorting the words of Jesus.'[3]

Since then, further work – for instance, by conferences in Pattaya (1980), Grand Rapids (1982) and Wheaton (1983) – established for many evangelicals the truth that the task of compassionate involvement in the needs of the world has a full justification of its own, based on the will of God and the compassion of Christ, independent of the evangelistic task. Now evangelicals too possessed a 'comprehensive approach' to mission.[4]

towards a definition of mission for today

Missiology as a discipline is, however, still struggling for coherence, and our era is characterized by confused definitions of mission. Academic conferences on the subject can be exciting but frustrating when speakers from widely differing standpoints sometimes operate with contradictory definitions of the task.

The task is diverse and complicated and consists of a number of elements and approaches. We need a way to assess the relative importance of each element, and a structure which will locate each in its proper place. My contention is that it is the centrality of Christ which must tie them all together and restore some order to the confusion. What follows is an examination of the four most prominent emphases in mission today, with an eye to the strengths of each but also to their inadequacy to take centre stage in our thinking.

The soteriocentric (salvation-centred) approach is a good name for the older evangelical emphasis. Salvation was about the future; Jesus saved from hell and promised heaven. Salvation was mostly personal, because sin is personal. The individual needed to be saved. This way of focusing the task of mission was a great driving force behind the faith-mission movement. Hudson Taylor was burdened above all else by the prospect of 400 million Chinese dying without Christ.

The proclamation of personal salvation is certainly fundamental to mission, and that salvation does have a major future element. Personal salvation is mission's primary goal, above even the alleviation of human suffering and social evil. Christ taught the priority of the eternal over the temporal, and the apostles clearly concentrated most of their effort on presenting Jesus as the one through whom we come, by faith, to reconciliation with God. In practice, we are rarely left with simple choices, and in many cases the alleviation of human suffering has to be chronologically prior.

To place individual personal salvation at the controlling and motivating centre of mission, however, is to weaken the task in two ways. First, in the past it has had the practical effect of making evangelism the justification for all the other elements of the task the church is called into the world to do. A mission agency starts a medical work so that it can tell the people about Christ. A church runs a playgroup so that it can bring in the mothers. But, as we have seen, these have a justification of their own in the compassion of Christ. Secondly, placing personal salvation at the centre makes human need the main motive of mission. But that place rightly belongs to the desire for the glory of God and the spread of Christ's lordship. We engage in mission primarily because we love God, and only secondly because we love our fellows.

The theocentric approach is summed up in the phrase *missio Dei*, the mission of God. The rise of this emphasis owes more to Karl Barth than to any other theologian. God the Father sends the Son; the Father and Son send the Holy Spirit; the Father, Son and Spirit unite in sending the church into the world. God is a missionary God and the church is an instrument in God's mission. Mission (God's work) is more important than missions (the church's work). So the church's task is not just to plant local churches; it is to engage with the whole range of God's turning to the world, to work out his purposes of love for the world.[5]

The great advantage of this approach is that it elevates mission above the church and sees mission as no less than a working out of God's purposes in this world. In fact, it has become so popular a concept that most theories of mission claim it for their own. This has meant that, in practice, *missio Dei* has often been used to define mission so widely that almost anything is mission, from supporting armed guerrillas in South Africa to protecting hairy gorillas in Zaire. *Missio Dei* has at times handed the agenda of mission over to the world, because if the church's task is seen as discerning what God is doing in the world and coming alongside to lend support, then the starting-point for our thinking about mission has to be what is happening in the world. An extreme form of theocentric mission has justified the death of evangelism on the ground that God is surely in all the major religions of this world.

The ecclesiocentric (church-centred) approach, like that of the soteriocentric, reaches far into the past. It sees both the task and the aim of mission as the establishing of churches. It was natural for Catholicism before Vatican 2 to view the task in this way, because the church was seen as the sole vehicle of salvation. A number of movements in Protestantism give a central role to the church (if not as the vehicle of salvation, then as salvation's ultimate objective). Older denominational societies often made it their aim to establish their brand of Christianity in every place regardless of other Christians already working in the situation. American missiologist Donald McGavran saw the growth of the church as the ultimate aim of mission, and the modern evangelical emphasis on church-planting, especially with the aim of creating a church in every 'people group', illustrates an ecclesiocentric approach.[6]

God's purpose is indeed to see his church planted among all peoples of this world. One difficulty, however, with placing the church as the central tool or aim of mission is that the interests of God clearly go wider than that. The idea of the kingdom of God is broader than that of the church, and should not be confined to it. God is at work in the world outside the church and in parallel to it. A second problem has been that of misplaced loyalty. Loyalty to our expression of the church has sometimes overtaken our loyalty to Christ himself, and we have often imposed a particular church's order and confession of faith on emerging churches across the world.

The anthropocentric approach sees understanding the people to whom we go as central to the task of mission. As David J. Hesselgrave states, 'For the first half of this century and beyond, the greatest impetus to the science of missions came from those who were informed by anthropology.'[7] This was particularly true of North American missiology. When the American Society of Missiology was formed, its journal *Practical Anthropology* was soon renamed *Missiology*. Anthropologists such as

Charles Kraft, Paul Hiebert, William Smalley, Eugene Nida, Jacob Loewen and Louis Luzbetak have been prominent in the development of missiology as a discipline.

The science of anthropology has given us valuable tools which have helped the task of mission immensely. But the movement has tended to neglect theology for sociology and anthropology. To place the understanding of people at the centre of the missionary task is to make a science of what is, rather, a crusade of love.

Christ as centre

If we place Christ at the centre, determining mission's content and motive, these other approaches fall into their rightful place and are assured of a vital role in the task. This Christocentric approach takes its cue from the Great Commission, which begins with Christ's declaration of his universal authority and continues with his command to extend obedience to that authority across the world (Mt. 28:18–20). It moderates the influence of the world on the agenda of mission and ranks the church as secondary to Christ. It in no way denies the importance of social and compassionate action, because, after all, these things were prominent in Christ's own ministry.

This model sees Christ as the exemplar, goal and content of mission, controlling it from the centre. Christ, sent by the Father, says to his church, 'As the Father has sent me, I am sending you' (Jn. 20:21). So we pattern our mission on his life and ministry. The goal is to please Christ because it is the love of Christ that compels us (2 Cor. 5:14). As C. T. Studd wrote, 'If Jesus Christ be God and died for me, no sacrifice can be too great for me to make for him.' And it is Christ who is himself the content of mission, not a set of dogmas. We present Christ as saviour and humbly seek to be Christ to a needy world.

the missionary society

Today's diversity in contemporary culture is also reflected in the way the church goes about its mission in the world. A Christian seeking to get involved will soon become acquainted with a whole string of initials representing missionary, evangelistic and support societies. The church has always needed agencies beyond the local congregation to help it fulfil its missionary task. As the church spread into Europe between the sixth and tenth centuries, particularly out of Ireland in the Celtic mission, it used the monks to great effect. A monastery would be planted in a pagan area and the monks would march down to the village, set up a cross in the middle of the square and begin to preach. In the great missionary expansion of the sixteenth and seventeenth centuries, it was the newly established orders, the Dominicans, Franciscans and Jesuits, which became the tools of the church's expansion. In the nineteenth and twentieth centuries, the characteristic tool has been the Protestant missionary society.

The first of these was the Baptist Missionary Society, founded in 1792 at the insistence of William Carey. The London Missionary Society, the first interdenominational body, was founded in 1795. The Church Missionary Society followed in 1799 and the British and Foreign Bible Society in 1804. Very few have died since then, and many more have been born. They were, and still are, effective tools for the task – although, with the advent of the Two Thirds World church and the ease of present-day communications, they need to rethink their role.[8]

competitive missiology?

It is instructive to note that the rise of the societies coincided with the rise of capitalist trade across the world from the West. The great trading-houses were very much in competition, and this infected the societies also. It has always been hard to remove that element entirely from them. Competition in the 'field' was greatly diminished (at least in Africa) by comity agreements, which gave each society a defined area in which to work. These have largely broken down today. More recently, grand co-operative ventures in Nepal and Mongolia help to offset the undignified rush for areas of ministry in parts of Eastern Europe after the fall of communism.

In the traditional sending countries, societies need supporters and candidates. Modern management methods have often been employed to set growth targets for individual societies, all of which draw money and people from a pool which does not grow any larger. Inevitably, one society's gain is another's loss. Expensive literature, display boards, attractive conferences and professionally designed corporate logos have all been used, and today's missionary exhibition does not look all that different from a secular trade fair. Today, new societies are springing up with all the speed and enterprise of new small businesses in society at large.

There are good things in this flush of diversity. A variety of interests can be more easily served by this entrepreneurial spirit in mission, and 'small is beautiful' economically. But it is also characterized by many of the disadvantages of a plethora of denominations. The societies are not sufficiently accountable to each other, their needless duplication makes poor use of the limited resources available, and they can generate a spirit of competition against which their personnel continually have to be wary.

None of this is intentional. The attitudes of consumerism and marketing are certainly far from the minds of most missionary-society personnel, and a great deal of selfless co-operation does take place, aided in Britain by the Evangelical Missionary Alliance and other organizations. But societies are battling with the impact of our pluralist culture, which has forced an unhelpful degree of diversity into what is at heart a useful system. We need to make a determined effort to change the culture of the missionary societies in order to create greater accountability between them, not only with regard to overseas operations but also with regard to the way they function in the sending countries. Whatever their beloved traditions, the societies must be willing to die or merge, if they are duplicating effort both at home and overseas. The aim of this would not be to produce 'multinationals', but simply to rationalize the situation.

finding our own way

The Christian response, however, must go beyond discussing the diversity of opportunity and actually get involved in the church's mission.

motive for mission

There is reason enough to do so. God is at work in this world, with a clear purpose to extend the lordship of Christ and confront darkness, evil, sin and suffering. He has invited every one of his people, indeed commanded us all, to participate with him in the task of mission.

Our own hearts also are beginning to be moulded after God's heart which feels something of the suffering in this world. We live in the West, most of us comfortably middle class, protected from many of life's pains by our society, family and friends, and screened from seeing the awfulness of others' existence by a usually selective media. Yet 4,000 babies die needlessly every day of poverty-related conditions, there are wars continually in some place or other across the globe, and the evil of human being against human being still beggars belief. Over all this lies the judgment of God on a sinful world, men and women who are without Christ and, as the apostle says, 'without hope and without God in the world' (Eph. 2:12). As we become aware of all this, compassion must move us into action.

guidance and subjectivity

We want to get involved, then, but by doing what, with whom, and where? Coping with today's diversities in mission gives rise to the question of how God guides us as we make decisions. Guidance is a comparatively new subject for evangelicals. As J. I. Packer[9] points out, the concern used to be holiness and now it is guidance; it used to be the general will of God for Christians and now it is the personal will of God for me. The shift has taken place because of the increased diversity of life. We live in a pluralistic society and, whereas society or family used to make choices with regard to the individual's job, marriage, travel, purchases and lifestyle, today the burden of choice is on the individual himself or herself.

This has led to an alarming subjectivity in how we seek God's will. Phrases such as 'God told me', or 'I feel that I ought to do this', are common. They are generally backed up by subjective appeal to the Bible in which verses are said to 'stand out' and thus become the voice of God for a specific situation or decision.

Such a subjective approach is dangerous. Feelings do not always come directly from God. Verses may well stand out because of factors in the reader rather than because of God. Isaiah 55:11, 'You shall go out with joy', will certainly stand out to a young man wanting to know if he should become romantically attached to a girl called Joy. But is it God speaking, or his own heart? Even the practice of laying out 'fleeces' (asking God for certain events to take place as an indication of his will) is remarkably open to subjective manipulation. After all, who defines the fleece?

the use of the mind

Sometimes the subjective approach is used as an excuse to avoid the necessary hard thinking involved in finding God's guidance. The mind is God's given instrument for taking decisions. We have no problem with this in the 'small' choices of life. Faced with diversity in the supermarket cheese cabinet, we simply follow our preference and work out which is the best buy. When we plan a journey, we make a reasoned choice about the best route. Yet the smallest choices can have consequences. By choosing one route, we may avoid an accident that happens on another. By choosing one type of cheese, we may pick up a listeria bug that was not present in others. In all such matters, we take the best decision possible and trust in the providence of God to protect us and achieve his purposes in our lives.

A similar process occurs when we decide how best to get involved in mission. We must use our minds to sort out the key factors on which the decision turns. A major factor is discerning the gifts God has given us. The question 'What should I be doing for God?' is far more important than 'Where should I be doing it?' It is better to restrict the idea of God's 'call' to the former. In a fast-changing world, we shall probably exercise our gifts in more than one place over the course of our lives. But what we should or should not do (wherever we go) depends on our individuality, especially our gifts, and the suitability of the role we may be asked to play. We must also think carefully about anything we feel may be God speaking directly to us. Clearly, he spoke to people directly in Scripture. God can speak in dreams, by giving us a burden for a particular group of people or task, or through giving others a word for us.

It is entirely appropriate, too, to think long and hard about where one can do the most good. A well-known illustration in mission circles is that of ten men carrying a log, nine at the light end and one at the heavy end. Where is help needed most? There are still many places in this world that are the heavy end of mission, with few to help. Not many are in the developed West.

the role of the Christian community

This emphasis on thinking the matter through must not be seen as individualistic. In the New Testament, the question of where one should go and what one should do in mission was decided corporately. Paul and Barnabas were sent out from Antioch after a decision taken jointly by the leadership group in the church. Even after Paul's vision of the men calling him to come over to Macedonia and help, the group concluded that God had called them to go (Acts 16:10). This group decision-making is wise, because individuals are emotionally involved in decisions about their own lives and futures. The participation of others dilutes the subjective element. To decide alone is to choose western individuality before the extended family of God.

The role of the church is particularly important in checking our thinking, in assessing together the truth of any direct word purporting to come from God, and above all in discerning our gifts or abilities and matching them with specific tasks. The church knows better than the individual whether that individual has (say) the gift of preaching. We may think of ourselves more highly or more negatively than we should. Others can see more clearly.

generosity and confidence

The lordship of Christ should inspire our willingness to go anywhere in the task of his mission. If I am a teacher, why not teach in central London? If I am an accountant, why not use my skills in Africa? If an evangelist, why not work in Thailand? Why not a lonely and hard situation? The 'why not?' questions are important if we are to give ourselves unreservedly to God. Our horizon of choice is often constricted by limited knowledge (which can be rectified), fear (which can be overcome) and the assumption that God wants us roughly where we grew up (which is often false). A daily and deliberate giving of ourselves to God without reservation places us in the right spiritual position to receive God's guidance.

We sometimes get anxious about guidance. It is like the fear of missing a plane. God has set down in heaven his perfect will for us individually, we think. It is difficult to find out, but we had better get it right or we shall miss it and end up with God's second best for the rest of our lives. That attitude, however, demeans God's care for his children. Certainly, if we refuse to do God's will when it is clear, we shall not receive his blessing. But the honest desire to please God is always rewarded. This fearful attitude also demeans God's sovereignty. Doubtless we make mistakes about what God wants us to do and where he wants us to do it, yet he takes up even our inadequacies and mistakes into the outworking of his will.

Our job is to do some prayerful hard thinking, along with the Christian community of which we are a part, and then get moving in the direction indicated with every confidence in a loving and sovereign God.

all because of Christ

Islam spread across the known world in the Middle Ages. Jerusalem fell in AD 638. Alexandria fell in 642, Persia in 650 and most of Spain by 715. But for Charles Martell at the Battle of Tours, all Europe would have become Muslim. Christendom responded in two ways. The Crusades sought to turn the tide militarily and kill as many Muslims as possible. With considerably more Christian spirit, Francis of Assisi and Ramón Lull sought their conversion.

Lull was a dissolute soldier-poet in the court of James I of Aragon in the thirteenth century when, while writing a love letter to his mistress, he received a vision of Christ crucified and was converted. He took seriously the need to understand Islam in order to evangelize its people, spending years studying Arabic and setting up colleges for the study of oriental languages and thought. He also took seriously the academic task and wrote an influential book of apologetics (unfortunately badly flawed). Above all, however, he served sacrificially, preaching and disputing in Muslim lands where he was imprisoned, banished, shipwrecked and eventually fatally stoned. 'Missionaries will convert the world by preaching', he wrote, 'but also through the shedding of tears and blood and with great labour and through a bitter death.' Doubtless thinking of his original vision of Christ crucified for him, he prayed: 'Men are wont, O Lord, to die of old age through the failure of natural warmth and excessive cold, but thy servant would rather die in the glow of love, even as thyself.'[10]

At the end, it is Christ who is the centre of mission and its motive.

confronting today's world

In many ways, we can heave a sigh of relief to find ourselves, as today's western church, largely back where we started in the New Testament era. After 1,500 years of the compromises and nominalism of various forms of the Christendom idea, we are again a minority, surrounded by pagans and facing up to religious plurality all around us. The turn of the millennium finds us in a classic missionary situation, with a gap opening up again between the culture of the Christian who seeks to proclaim Christ, and the world which needs Christ. Our agenda today, then, once more comprises the four fundamental tasks of mission: to understand, to say no, to put to one side our own cultural baggage, and to present Christ understandably, relevantly and in context.

starting with understanding

It has always been the view of effective missionaries that a comprehensive understanding of the people we go to is the essential foundation for mission. The amount of time William Carey spent translating much of the *Ramayana* into English, and writing and printing his elaborate Sanskrit grammar, was criticized by some of his supporters; but it showed how far he was willing to go to understand those he was trying to reach. Mission, as we have seen elsewhere, is not a matter of repeating the same words in every situation as if they were a magic spell. It means engaging genuinely with the situation. Otherwise we shall be heard wrongly or seen as irrelevant, both of which must be recognized as failures of faithfulness on the part of the missionary.

To understand, we have to engage in dialogue. Dialogue has been opposed by such disparate people as Martyn Lloyd-Jones and Karl Barth, on the ground that the church's duty in the face of unbelief is to proclaim rather than to engage in dialogue. But proclamation has to take place on the basis of understanding not only God's revelation but also the thought processes of the people to whom we proclaim that revelation. Dialogue has a long and honourable history in mission. Its first aim is to increase understanding by hearing from the other party exactly what they believe and why. Its second aim is to interact with those views from a Christian perspective.[11]

The only alternatives to such dialogue are either to withdraw from the attempt to communicate at all, or to shout at the world from a distance in words they cannot understand and with ideas they cannot appreciate – a sort of theological open-air meeting of the worst sort, with the preacher bellowing Christian jargon at people as they hurry past, taking away with them no more than the picture of a strange old man believing strange old things.

At a recent meeting of the World Evangelical Fellowship Theological Commission, Dr Ralf Hille of Tübingen claimed that it was this very attitude which brought about the defeat of the orthodox theologians at the hands of the liberals, and the loss of evangelical influence in universities, colleges and churches, in the last hundred years. Unlike liberal theologians, post-Reformation Protestant scholars erected strong, complicated theological systems which failed to interact in any significant way with trends in philosophical and sociological thought. They built castles on one side of the river rather than bridges linking the two (to use our metaphor from chapter 4).

The start of the process of mission to our society, with its complex mixture of modern and postmodern attitudes, is to understand it by dialogue with it. Increasingly, this dialogue with today's western worldviews is relevant across the planet. Every culture is unique, but the pace of westernization throughout the world is increasing. Modern communications are mostly transferring cultural symbols and attitudes from those who have control of the communications systems to those who receive them. And no Third World country can take the science and technology of the West without taking part, to some extent, in the attitudes which produced them and the West's present disillusionment with them.

saying no

One function of the gospel is to judge all cultures. Boniface, the eighth-century English missionary, arrived in Geismar, Germany, to preach the gospel. He took an axe to the town's sacred oak, dedicated to Thor, god of thunder, cut it down and built a chapel with the wood. It was a dramatic 'power encounter' between Christ and Thor. The tree fell, Boniface did not, and pagan religion lost. More than that, a missionary was saying that Christianity was incompatible with the belief system of the society at that point.[12]

We need to say the same. It is not possible to develop a critique of modern thought here, but I shall outline where and how I believe we need to confront some of the fundamental issues which are at stake. Some evangelicals are already doing that job, and their names are among those which feature below.

1. *We must disagree with the marginalization of God.* A number of recent thinkers take leave of the idea of a God who really exists, who created the whole world, who makes demands of it and who loves it. Friedrich Nietzsche declared that God was dead. Radical theologian Don Cupitt believes that God does not exist outside language about him. Others simply live their lives as if he did not exist. Pushed to give an answer, between 60% and 70% of the UK population still say they believe in God; but they live as if they do not. We need to reassert the message of Isaiah. In the face of idols and the enticements of localized gods, he declared the sovereignty of the one holy God over the whole world.

2. *We must address the inadequate way our society talks about truth.* We have already (chapter 1) discussed the idea that truth is relative, that nothing is true in itself or true for all. This notion must be confronted for three reasons. First, it is self-contradictory. If nothing is universally true, then the proposition 'Nothing is universally true' is not universally true; relativism dies by its own hand. Secondly, it has very dark consequences. Abolishing a standard of universal truth and morality means that nothing is universally false or always wrong. As Nietzsche saw, all that remains after that is the belief that 'might is right'. Most postmodern thinkers strenuously seek to avoid this conclusion, but it is there, logically, at the end of the slope. Thirdly, belief that truth is relative and local makes it difficult for Christians to uphold the biblical gospel as relevant for all people in all ages and contexts.

3. *We must resurrect the truth of history as recorded in the Scriptures.* The nature of history is a topic of live debate today. E. H. Carr's seminal book *What is History?* drew a distinction between history and the past. We have access only to history. Statements of what we call fact, such as 'The Second World War began in 1939', are valueless in themselves. 'History' is a network of interpretive frameworks built by less than objective observers. Therefore, Carr maintains, 'the concept of absolute

truth is also not appropriate to the world of history'.[13]

Christianity is not an enemy of subjective interpretation. The New Testament contains four gospels, each with its interpretation of Christ. Letters such as Romans and Hebrews supply distinctive interpretive frameworks addressing the meaning of his death. But we cannot allow Scripture to be treated as secular history. It is a historical record inspired by God and is therefore authoritative history, a concept anathema to the modern historian. We need to preserve the category of revelation, which is incompatible with relativism.

4. *We need to assert salvation through Christ alone.* Less than this is less than Christianity. Political correctness today frowns on such a claim to universal significance for Christ, and on proselytism – the attempt to persuade a member of another religion that he or she ought to become a Christian. We have to confront this as intolerance in the service of toleration, imperialism in the service of anti-imperialism. It is no more than late-twentieth-century western culture elevated to a position from which it judges all other views. Our task is to proclaim Christ as all and in all (Col. 3:11).[14]

These four issues (and others) are points at which Christian truth confronts our culture. Our task is to repute its errors convincingly.

shedding our Enlightenment baggage

When missionaries carry the gospel from (let us say) Britain to Africa, they must first of all divest it of the cultural baggage of their own society. They have a mandate to bring the gospel, but not to bring their culture too. This was not always understood in mission, and so we have Scottish Presbyterian church buildings in the heart of Nigeria, the Anglican Prayer Book and western hymn tunes in use among churches in Argentina, and western suits and clerical collars worn by preachers everywhere.

Similarly, when Christians step out into the modern world, we have every right to ask people to believe the gospel, but we do not have the right to ask our listeners to adopt evangelical cultural baggage. It has become increasingly plain that the cultural baggage of evangelicals today includes Enlightenment assumptions. This has recently been pointed out by David Bebbington, Dave Tomlinson and Alister McGrath.[15]

The thesis of David Bebbington, a British evangelical historian, is that evangelicalism as a historical phenomenon was actually launched on its way by the Enlightenment. There was a prior Protestant tradition in England, but this was remodelled under Enlightenment influence to produce evangelicalism as a new movement in the eighteenth century. Theologian Alister McGrath agrees, and points out that Enlightenment assumptions have influenced evangelicalism in at least four areas.

First, the way we have done theology has owed a great deal to rationalistic assumptions. Theology rightly admits a role for reason in the understanding of the faith. The Princeton school of Charles Hodge and Benjamin B. Warfield, however, adopted a scientific methodology and a logically consistent approach to theology which the Scriptures cannot bear. Hodge writes at the beginning of his *Systematic Theology*: 'We find in nature the facts which the chemist or the mechanical philosopher has to examine, and from them to ascertain the laws by which they are determined. So the Bible contains the truths which the theologian has to collect, authenticate, arrange and exhibit.'[16] Donald Bloesch traces this rationalistic approach to theology through other evangelical theologians of today, notably Carl F. H. Henry, John Warwick Montgomery, Francis Schaeffer and Norman Geisler. Against this approach, we have to assert that sometimes revelation appears to be logically inconsistent (for instance on the Trinity, the incarnation, election and responsibility), and we need to take a humbler attitude than Enlightenment rationalism allows. Furthermore, Scripture is not a source-book of doctrines so much as a narrative of the works of God.

Secondly, evangelical spirituality has been based on language and reason. It has concentrated on reading and understanding the ideas in Scripture and has downplayed any emotional and imaginative engagement with the text. This is the basis of the traditional 'quiet time' as taught to new Christians, and, says McGrath, it has had a devastating impact on evangelical spirituality, placing it at a disadvantage in relation to the spirituality of both Roman Catholicism and Eastern Orthodoxy. We need to recover what was common in the evangelical tradition prior to the Enlightenment: the importance of our wills, imaginations, feelings and bodies in our spiritual lives.

Thirdly, evangelical apologetics has largely operated within the Enlightenment paradigm of universal human rationality. D. A. Carson, of Trinity Evangelical Divinity School, asks us to imagine a student who majors in philosophy at an evangelical Reformed seminary. In a doctoral seminar with Paul Ricoeur, the student is plunged into consternation when his traditional apologetic approach does nothing to disable the 'principled pluralism and radical relativism' of the new thinking.[17] Universal categories of evidence and rationality are rejected *a priori* in much of today's academic world. Presenting a faith based on 'naked truth' will not meet the apologetic requirements of today's world.

Fourthly, our evangelism has betrayed its Enlightenment bias when it has sought to persuade people of 'the truth of the gospel' in the sense of propositional correctness. We have tended to proclaim the gospel (in that sense) and ask people to accept that, but it is Jesus Christ himself who is the truth. Faith is glad confidence in a person, rather than assent to the truthfulness of a set of propositions. Enlightenment pressures have sometimes led us to seek the wrong response.

assessing our Enlightenment heritage

Not all the Enlightenment influences on our faith should be regarded negatively. No-one wishes to return to a time, for instance, when the humanity (as well as the divinity) of the Scriptures was not recognized. Nor should we assess all the Enlightenment tendencies in evangelicalism as wrong. Some can be regarded as little more than a presentation of the truth in the thought-forms of the time, precisely the missiological task we are talking about. Some were attempts to meet fire with fire, as in the debate about Scripture. Dave Tomlinson describes the idea of inerrancy as a rationalist response to a rationalist attack, but fails to see that sometimes this kind of response is necessary. Both evangelicals and liberals have roots in the Enlightenment, and when they clashed on Scripture, they fought in the same field with similar armaments.

Nevertheless, to continue to present an evangelicalism built on Enlightenment assumptions and using Enlightenment terminology, at a time when Enlightenment attitudes are dying beneath us, is a classic missiological error. We must present a post-Enlightenment evangelicalism in a post-Enlightenment culture.

commending Christ in today's language

We have looked at the need to confront both our culture's presuppositions and the Enlightenment rationalism of our evangelical heritage. We must now ask how the gospel can be properly contextualized in our culture. This task understandably arouses fear. Roger Lundin, in a recent book on postmodern apologetics, warns that 'If Christians use postmodern vocabulary to communicate the gospel, the church will become the beast of burden ridden by postmodernism.'[18]

But what vocabulary *can* we use, other than that used by those we seek to reach? Paul Hiebert expresses a general missiological principle which he calls *critical contextualization*: 'Although the gospel is distinct from human cultures, it must always be expressed in cultural forms. Humans cannot receive it apart from their languages, symbols and rituals. The gospel must become incarnate in cultural forms if people are to hear and believe.'[19]

Western society on the threshold of the twenty-first century cannot be the only exception to this rule. As in every culture, there will be aspects which we must simply refute, as we have seen. There will also be categories and words which are seriously inadequate to express the truth. But this has always been the case in every language and culture. When such situations arise, we have to explain how we are using words, and what we mean or do not mean when we use particular symbols or concepts. But we cannot proclaim the gospel in a language different from that of our hearers.

Very little work has been done in this area to date. The movement towards alternative worship is one proposed solution which takes the need seriously. It is based on the following rationale. Although our society is no longer monocultural, the church unfortunately seems to be locked into that section of it which is the most traditional, representing the past and the thinking of older people. Young people, particularly students and professionals, think in much more postmodern ways and feel alienated by the traditional church. They need worship based on their own culture, with less emphasis on Enlightenment rationalism and a greater use (for instance) of images, signs, modern music and the celebration of creation. Sometimes enthusiasm has taken proponents of alternative worship into unacceptable territory, as when sexuality is celebrated in an erotic way as part of worship. But the desire to contextualize cannot be faulted. We need more, and more careful, experimentation in this area.

What we cannot allow is for such meetings to become churches. Donald McGavran of the 'church growth' school of missiology stated in 1970 that people 'like to become Christians without crossing racial, linguistic or class barriers'.[20] We should therefore aim to construct churches of 'homogeneous units' (that is, groups of people belonging to the same culture, race, class and language), since that is likely to accelerate the numerical growth of the church. But the church, even the local church, must be composed of all believers, whatever their culture. Jews and Gentiles belonged to the one New Testament church because barriers had been broken down by the gospel. If separate churches for black and white in South Africa are unacceptable, so are separate churches for traditionally minded pensioners and postmodern youngsters in England. The way to handle diversity in the church is not by creating more churches.[21]

In today's cultural context, then, apologetics in the sense of persuasive argument is difficult. If we appeal to biblical authority, it is not quickly recognized. Few non-Christians believe the Bible to be authoritative divine revelation, and most are quick to offer the view that science has shown the Bible to be inaccurate and very human. In any case, most are suspicious of the method that seeks to establish truth by authoritative pronouncements. Many will ask why the holy book of this particular religion should be regarded as truer than the holy books of other religions.

How are we to establish the legitimacy of Christian truth claims in such an atmosphere? Why should people listen? One solution increasingly recognized today is to make the truth visible in an attractive community.[22]

the church as the hermeneutic of the gospel

Rather than seeking to prove the objective truth that Jesus Christ is Lord, this view sees the first stage as showing the world what the lordship of Christ means practically in our lives. This presents Christ at the point where people are looking and in categories people can still accept. The church thus becomes the social base of which these truths are the plausibility structure. As Cardinal Suhard put it, 'To be a witness does not consist in engaging in propaganda, nor even in stirring people up, but in *being a living mystery*. It means to live in such a way that one's life would not make sense if God did not exist.'[23]

Mysteries provoke questions, as Peter's words suggest: 'Always be prepared to give an answer to everyone who asks you to give the reason for the hope that you have' (1 Pet. 3:15). To be the community which provokes hard questions in the minds of men and women today, we must be a certain type of church. I shall focus here on three key areas: the need to remove unnecessary offence; to become the attractive community the church ought to be in Christ; and to unravel the relationship between church, mission and power.

avoiding unnecessary offence

The cross will always offend. To believe in and trust ourselves to a person who died horribly two thousand years ago, moulding our whole life around him and his service, will seem foolishness in every age. We should not, however, put unnecessary stumbling-blocks in the way of those we invite to believe.

When the Jesuit Robert De Nobili arrived in Madurai in South India in 1605, a small church already existed there, founded by a previous missionary, Father Fernández. It was composed almost entirely of immigrants and was of a strongly Portuguese culture. The little church was boycotted and despised by the local people and so was missiologically sterile. De Nobili could do nothing with it, and so set about starting again. When he made a careful study of the culture and language of the Tamil people, he soon discovered that much unnecessary offence had been caused by the first church. He stopped eating meat and wearing leather shoes, obeyed purity rules, dressed appropriately, and in other ways showed his willingness not to offend. There is still a debate about some of the practices De Nobili allowed among his converts, but his church lived and grew.

This principle of removing needless offence from our churches for the sake of mission is thoroughly biblical. When the Jerusalem Council of Acts 15 ruled on Jewish practices in the church, it did so in order not to burden the converts beyond a few important requirements which would ensure that Jews, in turn, were not offended by the practices of Gentile Christians. Similarly, churches and missionaries in Muslim lands today abstain from alcohol and often remove their shoes when entering the church.

Are there elements of unnecessary offence which we should remove as we seek to witness to our culture? I believe so. First, the church often seems simplistic to those outside. It regularly proclaims Christ as the answer without a deep enough analysis of the questions. It was in response to this that John Stott published his ground-breaking book *Issues Facing Christians Today* (1984) and founded what is now the Institute for Contemporary Christianity. Today, a similar response is being made in the theological and academic area by scholars such as David Wells, Mark Noll and Alister McGrath.[24] Cliché-ridden preaching and predigested Sunday-school faith are an offence to many today. In particular, the simplistic certainty attached to the secondary issues which are reflected in denominational divides and bitter disputes, full of heat and little genuine intellectual light, is deeply unattractive to unbelievers looking at the church. The absence of peace and reconciliation smacks of hypocrisy.

Secondly, the church's prescriptiveness with regard to people's daily lives has often been a stumbling-block. Simplistic rules about what is right and what is wrong are often based on respectability rather than on holiness. We fail to see that much of the church's morality is conditioned more by culture than by the biblical text properly applied. Our attitude to secular culture is mostly composed of 'don'ts', and consequently we create a ghetto mentality in the church. Dave Tomlinson and others have presented this as a 'culture religion', brought about by a fusion of middle-class standards and Christianity. One wonders, however, whether this middle-class culture ever existed, or whether the church has instead created a middle-class version of the world as it would like it to be rather than as it is or ever was.

the church as the community it ought to be

When Christ ascended in about AD 30, he left a few hundred believers (Acts 1:15; 1 Cor. 15:6) including eleven close disciples. By AD 200, Tertullian could write: 'We are only of yesterday, but already we fill the world', and 'We have already penetrated all areas of imperial life – cities, islands, villages, towns, market places, even the [army] camp, tribes, palace, senate, the law courts. There is nothing left for you but your temples.'[25]

By AD 330, the emperor had declared himself a Christian, persecutions had ceased, Sunday was recognized as a day of rest across the empire, and soon the imperial army which had thrown Christians to the lions required every prospective soldier to be a Christian. In its first three centuries the church had conquered the empire.

Why did this happen? A number of factors were important. The Holy Spirit was mightily at work; the empire itself gave safe and easy passage for the gospel; it was a spiritually unsatisfied society. But the key factor noted by many historians was the simple attractiveness of the church. Despite its problems, it held out a prospect of hope to those who saw it, like a city on a hill seen by weary travellers. To the extent that it was true to its nature, it was a radical alternative to a society that failed to satisfy the deepest needs.

the attractive church

How does this work out today? Four characteristics of the church should shine out in our inadequate world.

First, we are a worshipping community. We meet Sunday by Sunday to sing and worship and declare our allegiance to God. Reverence and allegiance are not common in today's world. A society which believes it has come of age finds its own truth, lives for itself, and cannot understand worship. Yet each member of that society needs to heal his or her fragmented life with a great allegiance, a grand passion, a desire for God. This makes the idea of worship deeply attractive. Absolute commitment is rarely seen, but greatly respected when it is.

Secondly, we are a serving community. We live to minister compassionately to spiritual and physical need in the community. Julian, a pagan Roman emperor, was forced to admit that the early Christians fed not only their own poor, but the pagan poor as well. One result of the increasing individuality and subjectivity of our culture is that people find it hard to understand those who do not live for themselves. If there are no truths greater than oneself, there is no sense in self-sacrifice. When unbelievers see Christians living sacrificially and serving others, they want to ask why. This too is part of the attractive mystery of the church.

Thirdly, we are a loving community. Christ always intended his disciples to be known by their love for one another. It was one of the great attractions of the early church that, in a world of little love, here was a community of people committed to one another. We live in similar times. Mobility of the individual breaks up the extended family and long-term relationships. Selfishness, and the general wisdom that we must look after number one, damage deep committment. The fellowship of Christians, against this background, is profoundly attractive and elicits the question 'Why?' The answer is, once again, the gospel.

Fourthly, we are a proclaiming community by our very nature. We declare the gospel of salvation through Christ at every opportunity, lovingly but boldly. Proclamation is a mystery to our society because it does not easily fit into its opposition to claims that there is such a thing as universal truth – claims that seem to impinge on the liberty of others, such as the assertion that all need to be saved. Proclamation is not unattractive, however, if it is done responsibly and lovingly. While people may be impatient with simplistic certainty, especially with regard to lesser issues, most still sense a need to know true and false, right and wrong. People feel uncertain and insecure. To discover a church certain enough about something to proclaim it is sometimes like coming home.

Verbal proclamation of Christ – the story of our sinfulness, his work of salvation – the way back to God, and the life we were always meant to live as human beings – is the point we wish to reach with everyone. We cannot convey the full content of the gospel by our lives and deeds alone, and that is why the church has been commanded to proclaim it in words. It is just as well, because if the salvation of the world depended on the church mirroring the attractiveness of Christ, little progress would be made. But Christ, accurately presented, will always be more attractive than his church today and, by the Spirit, the gospel will always be the power of God for salvation (Rom. 1:16).

mission through weakness

One important area we must unravel for today is the church's relationship to power. To claim universal truth or morality is generally seen today as an unwarranted attempt to exercise power over others. Certainly, in the past, such claims have been used to enslave classes of people, and even in the history of the church the claim to universal truth has been used to justify torture, war, burnings, enslavement, imperialism and other uses of force.

Yet the church's mission does not have an automatic relationship to power, despite its basis in universal truth. Although God is all-powerful, the church is a location not of power but of weakness. It is on a pilgrimage, not a triumphant procession, and it is clad in rags, not crowns and jewels. The crown will come later when it is presented to Christ as his glorious bride. If the Bible is to be believed, God is not 'building a people of power', as the popular songs says, but using a people of weakness. Service for God has always been this way. The story of Gideon is a good example. He was the least of his family, from the weakest clan of an unexceptional tribe. He gathered together 32,000 men to fight the Midianites, but God reduced the number to 300. This calculated weakening of Gideon's position, states the narrative, was in order to open the situation to God and give him the glory (Jdg. 6 – 8).

It is a New Testament principle too. Paul was taught the same lesson. In terms of intellect, personality, commitment and spiritual experience, he was strong. Because of that, God weakened him. At first, he did not understand why, but, after pleading in vain for God to take away the 'thorn in the flesh', he hears God say, 'My power is made perfect in weakness.' Paul concludes: 'I delight in weaknesses … For when I am weak, then I am strong' (2 Cor. 12:7–10). It is a principle shining out from the ministry of our Lord; it was at the moment of his greatest weakness, while dying on the cross, that his greatest triumph was achieved.

This lesson, that God asks us to do mission from weakness rather than strength, has often been ignored. We use the language of conquest. 'Like a mighty army moves the church of God,' says the popular hymn, but it does not and it should not. We are not asked to conquer the world for Christ, or to be 'taking our cities for God' as a recent book was titled. We are called to go in humility and conscious weakness; to live out, albeit imperfectly, the life of Christ; to speak, albeit imperfectly, of his love and his salvation; and to leave the rest to his power.

conclusions

1. *We should not be seduced by romantic pictures of mission.* The picture of the pioneer missionary trekking through jungle swamps with a Bible under his arm is still occasionally true to life, but he is much more likely to travel by plane, and under his arm there may well be a notebook computer. We are about to enter the twenty-first century, and must not live as though we were still in the nineteenth.

2. *We must ensure that our compassion is as wide as God's.* God cares supremely that people should enter his kingdom and enjoy the richness of salvation now and for ever. This is our supreme concern too, but God also cares that the hungry should be fed, the orphans looked after, the sick healed, the brokenhearted comforted, the downtrodden lifted up and the exploiter brought low.

3. *We need to get involved.* There has been much discussion about the nature of mission, and this is right. The *International Bulletin of Missionary Research* uses a quotation from Elton Trueblood in its advertising: 'Those who believe in Christian mission have many tasks, but their first task is to think.' This is true, but it is only a beginning. God calls us to act. The question 'How am I furthering God's mission in this world?' deserves a practical answer.

4. *We must not do mission from an intellectual distance.* We need to understand, dialogue with and appreciate those to whom we wish to present the claims of Christ, not shout texts at them from a safe distance. There is nothing magical in a verse of Scripture. But when the Word of God is applied to a people in all their intellectual and personal struggles it carries all the power of the Spirit.

5. *Sometimes our duty is to confront and deny.* The gospel will judge all cultures and human constructions of reality. While we have a duty to express the truth faithfully in the forms of the culture where possible, in some areas all we can do is say no to those forms and redirect people to the alternative of the gospel. That too is faithfulness.

6. *We must be wary of our cultural baggage.* Whether we travel to Africa or talk to western non-Christian friends, we carry with us our own secular and evangelical culture which must not be confused with the gospel. We have a mandate to declare the gospel to all, and a duty not to confuse it with our own cultural expression of Christianity.

7. *We should present Christ in a way that is truly contextual, but preserve the unity and diversity of the church.* In our multicultural society, it can be useful to organize events (perhaps regular ones) that appeal to a particular

monocultural group, whether they be Chinese, men only, or young people. Yet the local church should be mature enough and secure enough to involve everyone, worshipping together and gathering together around the Lord's table.

8. *We must work to be the church we ought to be.* More than ever before, today's society needs to see the lordship of Christ in a local community before it considers the lordship of Christ as valid for them. Christ is Lord, regardless of anyone's attitude to universal truths. Nevertheless the love of a Christian community may well be the best initial commendation of the truth to a member of today's postmodern society.

9. *Refuse to speak from a position of human power.* From the Jesuits who bent all their efforts to the conversion of the emperor of China, to the Protestant missionaries in Africa who said, 'If only the chief were converted ...', mission has been done from a sense of strength. Political power, emotional force, position and intellect, have all been used in place of the power of the gospel itself. That has usually resulted in more harm being done than good.

10. *We should note the tragedy of today's church.* At just the time when it needs to be a winsome, united church for the sake of the gospel, it is often unattractive and divided. This is the theme of our final chapter.

6. unity

Nowhere is diversity and the Christian's need to choose more evident than in the multiplicity of churches. In 1982, David Barrett counted over 20,800 denominations belonging to 156 confessional traditions.[1]

New Christians are faced with bewildering choices. When they want to purchase, say, a new outfit, they can choose from a multitude of varied shops in the high street. It seems as though they have to perform a remarkably similar task in choosing between the many and varied churches in town. Perhaps only one church is right, but, given that they all claim to follow Christ, how can new Christians know which one? Perhaps they are *all* right, but then why are there so many varieties? Is it just a matter of choosing the one the individual likes best? Is the attitude that says 'The customer is king' the best way to find a church?

The disunity of the church is evident not only in denominational diversity. There are differences and alienations that cut across denominations. The charismatic movement, Reformed theology, views on the millennium, attitudes to the Bible, and many other issues divide Christians regardless of their denominational affiliation. These pan-denominational issues have produced a third level of diversity – regarding our attitudes to the diversity itself. Evangelicals, in particular, are now divided over which attitude to adopt to unity: should we simply work for unity among evangelicals (and, if so, on what criteria?), or should we participate in ecumencial moves towards unity between denominations?

In contrast to these divisions, the Bible speaks of one body of Christ, one flock because there is one shepherd, and of Christ's church in the singular. Following the pattern of preceding chapters, our task here is first to understand this diversity and its origins, and then to seek an approach to decision-making based on the centrality of Christ.

understanding the situation

The New Testament presents the church as a spiritual entity, the body of Christ, the creation of the Spirit. But it also sees the church as an identifiable, visible people of God which should manifest a visible oneness for the sake of the gospel. Such oneness demonstrates that Christ's disciples have been sent by the one God (Jn. 17:21) and bears testimony to the reconciling power of the gospel which breaks down dividing walls and makes warring human groupings one (Eph. 2:14–18). We have already seen that in the New Testament this visible unity did not require uniformity in all areas of belief and practice.

early attitudes to uniformity

The view that the visible unity of the church does require complete uniformity of faith and practice is usually a product of the desire to control. This was certainly true historically. When the Emperor Constantine, who converted to Christianity in AD 312, sought to reunite the Roman Empire, a new type of church came into being. Constantine used the church as a uniting force within the empire and imposed uniformity on it in order to do so.

This spirit carried over into medieval Christianity with all its prescriptions for liturgy, belief and practice. For instance, when the Synod of Whitby was convened in 664 to settle the controversy between the Northumbrian churches and those further south, the main points of disagreement were the date of Easter (Northumbria followed Irish custom, and the rest Roman) and the shape of the tonsure (Roman monks shaved the crown of their head while Celtic monks shaved the front). In reality the dispute was about who controlled the church.

Protestant principles

The traditional Roman Catholic view in the early sixteenth century was that because the Bible is difficult to understand, ordinary Christians need reliable and authoritative interpretation, and this was supplied by the church. It was Erasmus (later echoed by the English Reformer William Tyndale) who first claimed that every ploughman should be able to read the Scripture for himself. Luther in Germany and Zwingli in Switzerland agreed. 'The word of God,' said Zwingli, 'as soon as it shines upon an individual's understanding, illuminates it in such a way that he can understand it.'[2] The early Reformers believed that every Christian has not only the right to read and decide what the Bible says, but also the ability to do so. Its meaning is clear. This belief triggered translations of the Bible into the vernacular all over Europe.

This optimism, however, did not last long. The protracted controversy between the Reformers over the nature of the eucharist soon showed that honest Christians did not always come to the same conclusions about what the Bible meant. The Peasants' Revolt and the rise of extremists caused Lutherans and Calvinists to rethink the whole idea of Scripture's perspicuity. While still paying lip-service to these principles, they formulated statements of faith or catechisms through which the Bible should be read if it was to be rightly understood. But Pandora's box had been opened – after all, who constructs the statements of faith and on what basis? – and the march towards today's overwhelming diversity had begun.

modern attitudes

A number of tendencies in twentieth-century culture have reinforced ecclesiastical diversity. Foremost among these is our strong individuality in the West. We make our decisions. Society or family no longer decides for us. A consumer society both caters for and fosters this attitude, and we regard it as only reasonable that we should be given as wide a choice in religion as in so many other areas of life. The presence of various churches in one town supplies that choice which we regard as out right.

Coupled with the consumer's right to choose is the strong entrepreneurial spirit which, perhaps more in North America than in the UK, has led to the founding of new churches, denominations and evangelical movements on the basis of the 'vision' of one man or woman with little or no reference to the rest of the church. The coming of cultural variety in western nations, bringing with it the black churches and other expressions of Christianity new to the West, has also added to the diversity.

the ecumencial movement

The disunity of the church became a major issue from the early years of the twentieth century. Christians began to see that they were failing to present to the world the oneness of God, the nature of the church as the single body of Christ, and even the gospel of reconciliation. Resources were being wasted and our concentration turned inwards at a time when the world needed the united mission of the church.

The present ecumenical movement arose out of the World Missionary Conference at Edinburgh in 1910. From that great conference three streams emerged to continue the discussion: the Faith and Order movement, the Life and Work movement and the International Missionary Council. The first two merged on 23 August 1948 at Amsterdam to form the World Council of Churches, designed to bring churches and denominations together to talk about their differences under a minimalist statement of faith: 'The World Council of Churches is a fellowship of churches which accept our Lord Jesus Christ as God and Saviour.'[3]

The second Assembly of the WCC in New Delhi in 1961 was especially significant. The International Missionary Council was integrated, and the Russian Orthodox Church, formerly hostile, joined the movement. This Assembly adopted a more explicit statement of faith, which is still used by the WCC today: 'A fellowship of churches which confess the Lord Jesus Christ as God and Saviour according to the Scriptures, and therefore seek to fill together their common calling to the glory of the one God, Father, Son and Holy Spirit.'[4]

The ecumenical movement became the great talking point in Christendom. In Britain, local ecumenism often included Roman Catholic participation. There were Anglican observers at Vatican 2, and the first interconfessional talks between Catholic and Anglican theologians (ARCIC 1) began in 1970.

The Second Vatican Council of the Roman Catholic Church began in October 1962, and its nine sessions were to take it up to 1965. Council fathers shifted the emphasis away from the church as an institution towards the church as the people of God, which, they said, subsists in the Roman Catholic Church rather than being synonymous with it. The document also referred for the first time to Christians outside the Roman Catholic Church as 'separated brethren', and was positive about the prospect of their salvation.[5]

evangelical reaction

These developments produced varied reactions among evangelicals. One was outrage and condemnation. This was a move towards unity on too narrow a doctrinal basis, which threatened to wipe out the good done by the Reformation. The ecumenical movement was seen as bringing together true and false churches, unconcerned to distinguish between those who held to the inerrancy of Scripture and those on the liberal wing of the church. Other evangelicals, despite the problems involved, participated in the movement either individually or as a party within a mixed denomination.

Many evangelicals admitted the inadequacies of the solutions to disunity proposed by the ecumenical movement, but recognized the validity of the questions. Four major evangelical answers emerged, but they must not be seen as mutually exclusive, and individuals often belonged to more than one of these movements. These four answers can be regarded as the principal historical models for evangelical unity, and it is remarkable that they should all have been prominent and often in conflict on this issue in the 1960s. They can be represented by the Evangelical Alliance (a unity based on common action), the British Evangelical Council (a unity based on purity and separation), the Keele Conference (a unity based on denominational affiliation), and the charismatic movement (a unity based on common experience).

working together

The Evangelical Alliance was formed in 1846. Part of its aim was, and still is, to help evangelicals to take corporate action, whether evangelistic or social. Examples of this in the latter half of the twentieth century have included the setting up of TEAR Fund (The Evangelical Alliance Relief Fund), inviting Billy Graham to lead crusades, and lobbying Parliament on behalf of Christian values. In 1962 it issued a statement on ecumenism, acknowledging secondary issues on which Christians differ, but listing essential doctrines. Its list of essentials is much more comprehensive than that of the WCC. It went on: "To the extent to which churches (whether in membership of the WCC or not) fail to express these truths, to that extent they fall short of being churches in the New Testament sense, though individuals within them may be true believers.'[6] The EA has not, however, taken a position on particular denominations, and welcomes into membership churches and individuals in denominations fully engaged in the ecumenical process, as well as those outside it.

Not owned by, but actually reflecting the ethos of, the EA and its parent body the World Evangelical Fellowship, was the International Congress on World Evangelism, Lausanne, called by Billy Graham and held in July 1974. This was perhaps the most important moment of self-definition for evangelicals in the twentieth century. Once more, the form of unity envisaged was to be sought in joint action, especially mission, across denominational boundaries. The 2,700 participants returned from the congress to worship in their various churches, but with a renewed vision to evangelize together.[7]

the call to separate

On 18 October 1966, the belief that evangelical unity could be pursued without addressing the issue of denominations was shattered. Dr Martyn Lloyd-Jones, the influential minister of Westminster Chapel in London, was invited to speak at the public meeting of the National Evangelical Assembly. He put forward the thesis that, while separation from liberals was a duty, separation from fellow evangelicals was a sin. He therefore urged evangelicals to come out of their mixed denominations and join together. When he had finished speaking, John Stott, as chairman, immediately stood up to say that both history and Scripture were against what Lloyd-Jones had said, and appealed for no-one to act precipitately.

The meeting was polarized and evangelicalism was deeply divided on the issue from that evening.[8]

The British Evangelical Council was revived to act as an umbrella organization for those churches and denominations which took this anti-ecumenical stance and, by 1981, it represented more than 2,000 congregations. The Westminster Fellowship, an interdenominational gathering of ministers hosted by Lloyd-Jones, adopted a clause requiring members to be in sympathy with this position. A number of nonconformist churches withdrew from the EA. The division among evangelicals over secession continues to this day. It must be regarded as a tragedy that Lloyd-Jones's appeal for greater and closer unity among evangelicals resulted in greater suspicion and disunity among evangelicals overall.

staying in

Just six months after the dramatic call to leave mixed denominations, in early April 1967, the first National Evangelical Anglican Congress was held in the University of Keele. Once again, the ubiquitous John Stott was chairman. The congress produced a declaration which stated that evangelicals in the Church of England took delight in being Anglican, and included the phrase, 'We desire to enter this ecumenical dialogue fully.'[9] This desire to walk together and learn together with others within the denomination marked a new direction for evangelical Anglicans, and the start of a growing and exuberant evangelical revival in the established church. A similar, though later, revival of evangelical interest can be seen in the Baptist denomination, which, in the 1960s and 1970s, was second only to the Church of England in providing a home for evangelicals.

One key proponent of the view that evangelicals should remain within their denominations was J. I. Packer. An Anglican minister, he was, until the disruption of 1966, a member with Lloyd-Jones of the Westminster Fellowship and the Puritan Conference. In the 1960s he was prominent in the evangelical opposition to plans for union between the Methodist and Anglican churches, and in discussions between evangelicals and Anglo-Catholics which resulted in the controversial book *Growing into Union* (1970). He became a rallying-point for non-secessionist evangelicals.

one in the Spirit

The 1960s saw the coming of the charismatic movement to Britain. It transcended denominations, and was never confined to traditional evangelicalism. A 1977 report of discussions between charismatics and non-charismatics in the Church of England concluded that 'we share the same evangelical faith',[10] and this was disconcertingly echoed by an enthusiastic Scottish Roman Catholic bishop who noticed that when a Catholic young person experienced the charismatic renewal it usually gave him 'something of the evangelical emphasis on Jesus as his personal saviour'.

Michael Harper, at that time John Stott's curate at All Souls, Langham Place, was an early and influential leader of the British charismatic movement. He and others welcomed the interdenominational character of the movement on the grounds that common experience of Jesus and the Holy Spirit transcends the old traditions. The feeling was that God was doing a new thing. Large charismatic conferences, for instance under the auspices of the Fountain Trust which Harper founded, regularly drew charismatics from all the major denominations, including the Roman Catholic Church.[11]

This uniting movement, also, became a significant cause of disunity. It polarized those who believed it to be of God and those who did not. Individual congregations up and down the country were split, and evangelicals took sides. The rise of Spring Harvest, and other large events which have seen charismatics and non-charismatics co-operating, pointed to the acceptance, by the 1980s, of the need to live together. But this co-operation is still by no means universal.

evangelical unity in the 1990s

Currently, a lethargy has settled on evangelicalism with regard to visible unity. All past efforts to promote it have resulted in greater disunity. Would it not be better to accept the denominations as necessary, even desirable? Our job, surely, is to root out a sectarian spirit and wait for the Lord to sort out the mess when we all get to heaven. Three recent books well express this concentration on our attitudes to one another: *One in the Truth* by Robert Amess (1988), *Evangelical Reunion* by John Frame (1991) and *One Lord, One Faith* by Rex Koivisto (1993).[12]

Amess's book is a warm appeal to abandon suspicion and sectarianism and to be willing to change one's mind. He is of the opinion, however, that deeper disputes – such as those about baptism, and Reformed *versus* Arminian theology – will never be resolved. John Frame's book examines denominationalism, pointing out how it has damaged the idea of the church and encouraging us to see full unity as our eventual goal. As a Presbyterian, he welcomes the merging of similar denominations where possible. But he too is not hopeful of great change, and devotes his final chapter to the issue of developing better attitudes to other Christians.

Koivisto's book is the boldest. For him, denominations are not only inevitable but, in fact, the best way to express the catholicity of the church, because they preserve the vital element of freedom of choice. He believes (against all history) that they protect against sectarianism on the one hand and latitudinarianism (the minimalizing of doctrine and ecclesiastical practice in the interests of tolerance) on the other. He takes the model of the 'city church' from the British scholar H. L. Ellison: the local church in city X comprises, in biblical terms, all the gospel-believing congregations in that city – just as the local church in Rome in Paul's day met in several house congregations. Koivisto limits his vision simply to greater co-operation in such situations.

As we approach the new millennium, those in the ecumenical movement are disillusioned and frustrated, and evangelicals who opposed it are as far from unity as ever. While often enjoying fellowship together in big events and interdenominational societies, they are resigned to returning to their different churches each Sunday. It is a particularly embarrassing problem for evangelicals. The casual observer would doubtless note some incongruity in the fact that the group which claims loudest and longest that it alone has the gospel of reconciliation in its fullness is, of all Christian groupings, the least reconciled within itself and the most sectarian in its attitude towards its fellow members. As Gilbert Kirby, a former president of the Evangelical Alliance, said in 1984, the quest for unity is an honourable one and, despite setbacks, must go on.[13]

the problem of theology

But is it not the case that all these divisions arose because of genuine theological differences? Surely the only way to become one is in the truth?

what is truth?

We are already in a good position to address the question of our theological differences. We noted in chapter 1 that our pluralistic society presents us with a variety of choices about what to believe. It sees freedom in matters of faith as a good thing, and it often regards religious truth as simply a question of culture – something may be true for an individual or group, but not universally true. Indeed, postmodernism is suspicious of all 'metanarratives', or claims to universally true truth.

We rejected this notion that belief is culturally relative and found, in chapter 2, a firm base for our faith in Jesus Christ as he is revealed in the Scriptures. Yet, in subsequent chapters, we went on to note two things.

First, some of our disagreements in theology are of cultural and historical origin and not simply a matter of different interpretations of the Scriptures. To take just one instance, our doctrines of church structure were shown to have originated at least partly in the prevailing social structures. As H. Richard Niebuhr, the noted writer on the church and culture, observed, 'the relationship of these forms to the political experience and desire of various groups is considerably more pertinent than is their relation to the New Testament.'[14]

Secondly, it is not enough to recognize the bare fact that although the one Bible is our standard for all doctrine, we interpret passages differently. We have to go deeper and ask why we do so. This leads us to see that culture and historic doctrinal traditions act as filters when we read the Bible, predisposing us to a particular interpretation.

the accommodation of God

What is God's attitude to all this? He in fact seems willing to accommodate himself to our weaknesses and differences.

The word 'accommodation', in the jargon of missions, refers to a practice whereby missionaries allow and accept the distinctives of the host culture within the new church so long as they do not damage the gospel. The most famous controversy surrounding it arose when the Jesuit missionary Matteo Ricci, working in China towards the end of the sixteenth century, permitted his converts to continue, among other practices, the placing of food in front of ancestral tablets. He argued that it was not idolatry and, in any case, western Christians put flowers in front of their 'ancestral tablets' in graveyards. The appeal against the practice by the Dominican Order was nevertheless eventually accepted in Rome, after a century and a half of dispute.

God seems to have a similarly accommodating attitude to lesser differences among Christians. George Whitefield was a strong Calvinist; John Wesley was equally committed to his Arminian principles. God used both men widely in the Great Awakening of the eighteenth century. Charles Haddon Spurgeon, strongly of the Baptist persuasion, was greatly used by God in the second half of the nineteenth century in England, as was John Charles Ryle, an Anglican bishop and a stout defender of infant baptism. In the church today, godliness is obviously not confined to any one party, whether charismatic or non-charismatic, or premillennialist, postmillennialist or amillennialist, but individuals from all groupings are close to God and greatly used by him. 'These facts are deeply instructive ...' comments E. J. Poole-Connor, writing about the 1859 revival in Ireland; 'they show that in many matters on which we are accustomed to lay stress, His ways are not our ways nor His thoughts our thoughts … God wrought as impartially through the "traditional churches" as he did through the Brethren assemblies, and the human distinctions between Anglican and Dissenter, Presbyterian and Independent, Baptist and Paedo-Baptist, seemed in that great day of visitation, to be as little more than the preoccupation of children.'[15]

This is not to claim that such differences are of no account. It is to assert that God does not regard them as sufficiently important to justify his rejection of one party or the other, or to require individuals or groups to change their views on these issues before he blesses or uses them.

the division of doctrine

Some (but not all) doctrines can be placed in this category of matters too small to rank among God's priorities for his people. A comparison of two New Testament passages will make this plain.

In Romans 14, Paul asks Christians to accept one another without disputing about opinions and passing judgment on one another. Whatever they believe about certain practices of others, they are to keep it to themselves and love those with whom they disagree. In Galatians 1, however, Paul has a different message. He is astonished that the believers in Galatia are deserting Christ. Those who are leading them astray by preaching 'a different gospel' are eternally condemned.

Both passages focus on the continuation of Jewish ceremonies and rules in the Christian church. Romans 14 discusses lesser matters, such as the observance of special days and the eating of unclean foods, which are not relevant to the kingdom of God. But Galatians 1 is reacting to a group of people who believed that the Jewish rite of circumcision was essential to salvation, implying that Christ's work on the cross was insufficient. Some beliefs or doctrines are clearly more important than others.

We must therefore speak of a distinction in doctrine between those truths at the centre, part of the gospel, and those truths that do not matter so much to God or the church. The distinction between two categories of truth, labelled *fundamenta* (the fundamentals) and *adiaphora* ('things indifferent'), was developed around the time of the Reformation. Calvin, for instance, quotes Philippians 3:15, 'All of us who are mature should take such a view of things. And if on some point you think differently, that too God will make clear to you.' He continues: 'Does this not sufficiently indicate that a difference of opinion over these non-essential factors should in no wise be the basis of schism among Christians?'[16] Similar views were shared by Luther and other Reformers. Erasmus writes of those things he does not class as articles of faith: 'For these questions, which are a commonplace theme of scholastic debates, I would not dare to take a man's life if I was judge nor to risk my own life.'[17] The concept was developed in later Lutheranism and became a tenet of the Anglican church.[18]

Roman Catholicism and the hierarchy of truths

There is some evidence (collected by Yves Congar in his book *Diversity and Communion*) that the idea of divisions of doctrine into matters of greater and lesser importance was not unknown throughout the history of the Roman Catholic Church. But the generally received view was that it could be applied only to the most inconsequential ceremonies. Pope Pius IX, writing in 1865, is plain: 'As to the dogmas of faith, it is a quite illegitimate distinction: it is the distinction which some have thought fit to introduce between articles of faith which are called fundamental and others which are called non-fundamental articles of faith, some being accepted by all, and the others being left to the free assent of the faithful. Now the supernatural virtue of faith has as its formal object the authority of the God who reveals, an authority which does not allow of any distinction of this kind. That is why all the true disciples of Christ believe, for example, in the mystery of the august Trinity with the same faith as in the Immaculate Conception, in that of the incarnation of our Lord and in that of the infallible *magisterium* of the Roman pontiff.'[19]

This is, of course, understandable in principle (though Protestants cannot accept Pius's application) if we regard truth simply in logical terms: one truth is no more or less true than another. It is also a natural position for those who see the church as defining truth, because any one definition is just as much defined as another.

If we think of truth as truth *about* someone (Christ), however, there is more room for a hierarchy of truths, none of them less true than others, but some of them more significant. This perception caused a shift of attitude on the issue at Vatican 2. Its decree on ecumenism (21 November 1964) points out that 'When comparing doctrine with one another, they [Christians of other churches] should remember that in Catholic doctrine there exists an order or "hierarchy" of truths, since they vary in their relation to the foundation of the Christian faith.'[20] Carrying forward the thought of this decree, Congar envisages theology as a great tree; even the furthest twig is part of the organic whole, but some branches are more closely connected to the trunk and so more essential to it.

Similar pictures have been suggested by evangelicals. Some find value in the idea of concentric circles, with some truths nearer the centre and others towards the periphery. This enables us to distinguish between, for instance, baptism, which many would place close to but not among the fundamentals, and the timing of the Lord's return, which many would see as of lesser consequence. Some issues certainly create more difficulties than others for Christians, and several, while not fundamental, can still cause injury to some Christians. But when a church decides whether to offer fellowship to another person as a fellow Christian, we cannot avoid distinguishing between doctrines. We accept one another on the basis of the fundamentals, and talk together about the secondary issues of the faith.

C. H. Spurgeon once famously stipulated, 'First purity and then unity, first truth and then oneness.'[21] This is the right order, but we need to define purity and truth carefully. It is clearly unbiblical to require agreement on every interpretation of the Word of God regarding even the smallest issue before extending the hand of fellowship. If we see purity and truth as relating to the fundamentals rather than to the secondary issues, however, then these are required of every church and believer. A person who disagrees with a fundamental of the faith must be regarded as a heretic and so is not eligible for Christian fellowship, although still a recipient of Christian love.

sorting out the fundamental issues

In January 1527, Felix Manz, an Anabaptist, was put to death by drowning in the River Limmat after one of the great Reformers, Huldrych Zwingli, said, 'Let him who talks about "going under" go under.' Other Reformers similarly persecuted the Anabaptists for their rejection of the validity of infant baptism.[22] Yet most evangelicals today would not consider the mode and timing of baptism to be of fundamental importance. Perhaps even the content and size of the list of fundamentals have cultural and historical determinants. Examples such as this raise the issue of how we decide which doctrine goes in which category. Historically five tests have been used to determine whether an issue is fundamental.

The first is the test of *scriptural attestation* — not whether Scripture teaches the doctrine or not, for this would leave the matter open once more to dispute, but whether the Scriptures teach it as a fundamental of the faith. For instance, the doctrine of the person of Christ is mentioned as a test of fellowship in 2 John 7–12. Other fundamental doctrines are listed in Ephesians 4:4–6.

The second test is that of the *antiquity* of the doctrine. Some look for the consensus of the early fathers; others are happy to use the Apostles' Creed, as being a statement of the faith of the earliest post-canonical church. The *consensus quinquesaecularis*, or the statements of the first four ecumenical councils in the first five centuries of the church, is the basis adopted by a number of Anglicans. Of course, the consensus of the early church is valuable, but it is difficult to decide where to stop. Why not include the seventh council, the Second Council of Nicaea, in 787, which authorized the veneration of icons? Neither is this test alone adequate, since, as new heresies arise, they need to be rebutted. Nevertheless, there is real usefulness in this test. The earliest councils are universally accepted by Christians and few would refuse to use the Apostles' Creed in their worship.

Thirdly, there is the test of *universal consensus*. This is expressed well in Richard Baxter's famous aphorism (although it certainly pre-dates that great Puritan writer): 'In necessary things, unity; in *doubtful* things, liberty; in all things, charity.'[23] Taken on its own, the test is a circular argument, since it uses those things on which Christians agree to define Christians. Alongside other tests, however, it is useful. There are issues of theology over which Christians have invariably disputed. However plainly each side thinks the Scriptures speak on these matters, the fact that each has, in every age, found biblical support demonstrates the difficulty of interpreting the Bible in these areas.

The fourth test is that of *soteriology*, or the 'Bucer principle'. Martin Bucer was prominent in seeking agreement among the Reformers, and proposed that fundamental truths were those doctrines 'necessary to be believed for salvation'. Following him, the Thirty-nine Articles of the Church of England distinguish between those things necessary for salvation and those not, forbidding the church to require belief in the latter (Articles VI and XX). This criterion is dangerous if it is taken to imply that we gain salvation simply by believing those necessary things. We are never saved by believing doctrines, even the doctrines of the gospel. We are saved by faith in Christ himself. What is more, we should never demand that a person fully understand these essential doctrines before we accept the reality of his or her conversion. God can graciously save those not entirely in the truth, so long as they are entirely trusting in Christ.

Nevertheless, this test is useful because there is a basic body of doctrine which the church is charged with proclaiming throughout the world. It concerns Christ, his life, death and resurrection, his lordship, and his salvation of all who come to him in faith. It is the content of the early preaching of the apostles, and what evangelicals call the gospel. Any 'gospel' other than this is no gospel, and merits eternal condemnation (Gal. 1:6–9). Erasmus, as we saw, was unwilling to risk his life for secondary issues; but for these gospel truths we are willing to lose our lives.

The fifth test concerns the *consequences* of believing this or that view. Does it make a genuine difference to the holiness or spiritual life of believers one way or the other? In the twelfth century, the churches of the East and the West divided over the doctrine of the 'double procession' – whether the Holy Spirit 'proceeds' from both the Father and the Son (as the western churches held) or from the Father only. Some recent Eastern Orthodox writing has been applying this fifth test to this question. Sergius Bulgakov comments that 'In practice the two parties ... cannot prove the difference in their veneration of the Holy Spirit, despite their disagreement over the procession. It would appear very strange that a dogmatic divergence of such apparent magnitude should have no practical repercussions when normally dogma always has a practical importance and determines religious life.'[24]

This test echoes the words of our Lord when he talked of good trees bearing good fruit and bad trees bearing evil fruit: 'By their fruits you will know them.' We are asking not whether one belief rather than another is marginally better for the Christian's life and walk, but whether godly, spiritually alive believers are found on both sides, or one, or neither.

The task of separating the fundamental issues from the secondary by means of these guidelines is certainly not impossible, and some modern statements of faith, such as those of the Evangelical Alliance, the UCCF, the Lausanne Congress and some of the interdenominational missionary societies, have done a good job. Others have been less successful, mixing up fundamental and secondary issues in one confession. They thus bar many believers from fellowship with them, making their grounds of acceptance narrower than God's and their church more exclusive than Christ's.

mystery

Theology is a human attempt to explain, for a specific group of people, the character and acts of a God who is beyond comprehension. Language is seldom adequate for this task; illustrations from our this-worldly lives can be no more than partly true. Theological statements may appear to be logically impossible, as when we say that God is three yet his oneness is undamaged, or that God elects to salvation yet human beings remain responsible for their choice.

The inadequacy of a rationalistic Enlightenment view of reality, which left little room for mystery, was questioned early in the twentieth century. In 1927, at the International Congress of Physics at Como, the Danish physicist Niels Bohr introduced the concept of 'complementarity' – that natural phenomena can be looked at in mutually exclusive ways, as when subatomic particles are seen to behave both as particles and as waves. From this he extrapolated an epistemological principle: 'The opposite of a true statement is a false statement, but the opposite of a profound truth can be another profound truth.'[25] Given the level of mystery inherent in divine revelation, this offers a useful way of recognizing the truth on both sides of some of the major theological fences.

Acknowledging this mystery drives us to humility. We cannot tie God down to our systems; we cannot set out the full truth on every issue in a form of words that commands universal assent. God is too big for that. Acceptance of one another and a desire for greater unity, therefore, often derive from a high view of God, while a refusal to move towards one another can often stem from theological pride.

Acknowledging this mystery also inspires a desire to go deeper in the search for resolution. Perhaps there is a layer of understanding below the layer of disagreement, and perhaps it is accessible to the human mind. Maybe when we get there we shall be able to agree. One example is Jürgen Moltmann's work on the 'double procession' controversy, in which he probes behind the use of words on each side (Latin and Greek) to find substantial areas of agreement.[26] This approach has to be distinguished from much early ecumenical practice which merely tried to find a set of words which could be interpreted so as to satisfy all sides, and so succeeded only in papering over the cracks.

the church catholic

Although we have dealt at some length with the theological issues relating to unity, we must bear in mind that the church is more than theology. Our western, analytical culture, influenced by the Enlightenment, would place precise doctrinal formulation higher on the agenda than most other societies around the world. We must therefore take account of the nature of the church as we seek its unity.

evangelical catholicity

Some years ago, a provocative advertisement for a new journal depicted one man whispering to another, 'Hey, want to learn how to be more catholic without being less evangelical?' It was part of a movement in the United States back towards the episcopal church and a sense of history. Many were becoming tired of the simplistic and rationalistic tendencies of contemporary evangelicalism, and Englishmen such as C. S. Lewis, John Stott and J. I. Packer represented a depth and tradition which much of North America longed for. Two individuals stand out in the movement: Robert Webber, a Baptist lecturing at Wheaton College, who became an Anglican, and Donald Bloesch, a theologian at Dubuque Theological Seminary in Iowa. The latter wrote in 1978: 'Evangelicalism and Catholicism are two themes in the Christian symphony, and Christianity, biblical Christianity, is not complete without either of them.'[27] Those who were brought up on the glories of the Reformation and who equated catholicism with the Roman Catholic Church, however, found the whole idea disturbing.

what is catholicity?

Catholicity is one of the four marks of the church enshrined in the creed arising out of the Council of Constantinople in AD 381, the others defining the church as one, holy and apostolic. It comes from the Greek *katholikos*, which means 'general' or 'universal'. It can also denote 'completeness', the interpretation favoured by the Orthodox churches. Soon the church used this adjective to distinguish itself from the heretics and schismatics, so giving catholicity a theological nuance. Nowadays catholicity is sometimes used to affirm the church as a society for all races, peoples and cultures, and the ability of the church to speak in all languages and thought patterns, with relevance for every people.

We can distinguish between two types of catholicity. First there is a geographical catholicity: the one church is spread across the world and is found in all nations, in so far as they have heard and responded to the gospel. Secondly, there is a historical catholicity: the whole church spans the ages, from the apostles until today. It is this historical catholicity which causes problems for evangelicals.

We have tended to write history from a 'remnant' perspective, seeing the church not just as the faithful remnant surrounded by the world, but also as the faithful remnant within the wider church, the true church within the false. We have regarded the New Testament church as relatively pure but, soon after the apostles, increasingly corrupted by innovations and false doctrine, especially after the conversion of Constantine. There then followed more than a thousand years of darkness (which, incidentally, is often referred to within Roman Catholic circles as the 'Age of Faith') until the light returned in the Reformation. Liberalism, however, soon captured most of the Protestant church; yet a remnant remains, waiting for the Lord to return and vindicate its stand. Most of the church has been wrong about most of the important things for most of its life.

tradition

In such an atmosphere, built to a great extent on ignorance, it is easy to reject church traditions.

The Roman Catholic Church ranks tradition on a par with Scripture as one of the two parts of revelation. This was confirmed by Vatican 2: '... both Scripture and Tradition must be accepted and honoured with equal feelings of devotion and reverence ... sacred Tradition and sacred Scripture make up a single sacred deposit of the Word of God, which is entrusted to the Church.'[28] In particular, tradition is regarded as an important interpreter of Scripture. The Reformers protested against this twin model because it had led to tradition *controlling* Scripture. They contended for the Word of God as *sola Scriptura*, Scripture alone.

Yet it must be admitted that evangelicals have evolved traditions which pose at least an equal danger, since they are often allowed to control the way we read the Bible. We cannot banish tradition, because we cannot come without presuppositions to the Word of God. We read the text through the filter of that body of doctrine and practice we have been taught. We can do no more than be aware of the process, and seek to read as honestly as we can, with the help of the Holy Spirit.

worship

Nowhere is the importance of history seen more clearly than in our worship. Christians worship in many different ways. This diversity in forms of worship has cultural roots, with different cultures naturally tending towards different forms. In Africa, the mission churches' attempts to maintain the traditional hymn sandwich and keep worshippers in their pews without any undue movement of the body has now resulted in a breakout of African exuberance. This is mostly outside the traditional denominations, in the African independent churches, but nowadays is found even within churches whose names we recognize in the West. Where else do Presbyterians dance?

Diversity of worship also has roots in personality differences among worshippers. People join churches where they feel 'at home'. Some of us find it easier than others to show our emotions in public, and usually choose a church accordingly. Finally, this diversity has historical roots.

Churches have different worship traditions, whether codifed in a praye book as in the Anglican churches or left in an unwritten constitution a among Baptists.

In this sense, all worship is liturgical, but the word 'liturgy' usuall refers to the historic structures of the service, the use of the Christian yea in determining the content of worship, and set forms of prayer and praise There are elements of liturgy embedded in the New Testament, and number of practical arguments for its use. After all, most of us would prefer to be led in prayer occasionally by the great and good Thoma Cranmer than by a youngster fresh from college. The classical argumen for liturgy, however, is that of historical continuity, or catholicity. Liturgy gives the worshipper a sense of belonging to the church of all ages as wel as to the church of today. G. K. Chesterton commented that liturgy is the most democratic form of worship, for it allows one's great-grandparent to have a vote in what one does today.[29]

Yet there are also examples of spontaneous, open worship in the New Testament. We therefore need a generous spirit and a willingness to lear from one another. Those accustomed to liturgy can learn a great deal fror the spontaneity and variety of other forms. Those used to open, spontaneous worship can learn a great deal from the richness of the historica forms.

When Christians from different traditions or with different preferences come together, they face a strong test of love. They need to give place to one another in this matter, happy to see others given a vehicle for worship which makes it possible for them to pour out their hearts in worship to God without hindrance. In return, they hope for similar consideration from the others. Such services must contain a variety of forms This kind of approach is infinitely better than holding two types of service for the same local church, and so proclaiming incompatibility in the body of Christ. There is no support for such separation in the New Testament.

the regulative principle

But should the Bible determine the form of worship more precisely? This question brings us into debate with the 'regulative principle' adopted by the English Puritans of the seventeenth century. It finds its roots a little earlier in the continental Anabaptists and in William Tyndale and John Hooper at the time of the English Reformation. Iain Murray sums it up in two propositions: (1) everything introduced into the church without scriptural sanction is unlawful, and (2) the form of the visible church in the

New Testament is permanently binding on all generations of Christians.[30] Each element of worship must therefore be either explicitly proposed by the New Testament or required by logical deduction from a passage of Scripture. The principle was not, of course, applied to incidentals such as the times of services, but to everything which had a spiritual significance or was a part of worship itself. Historically, this principle drove the Puritans to secede from the Church of England. If they had stayed in, they would have been required as ministers to wear vestments, as communicants to kneel for the reception of the sacrament, and as theologians to compromise their belief that presbyterian church structure is the only divinely instituted form. Today, the application of the principle manifests itself among for instance, Covenanter Presbyterians, who refuse to allow musical instruments in worship, or hymns composed after the close of the canon of Scripture.

Those who advocate the regulative principle do not deny that some issues are fundamentals and others are things indifferent. But they create a category between these two: matters which, even though they are not essential for salvation, are plain in Scripture and so binding on the faithful. They are part of God's ordering of his church and, if they are neglected, serious results can be expected.

Nowadays, when people seem to construct their worship in a way designed to suit themselves and for their enjoyment, the regulative principle is a firm reminder that when we worship, our only aim should be to please God. It must be said, however, that there is no New Testament evidence for a uniform church structure and a single form of worship among all the churches of which it speaks. Nor could the Puritans agree entirely on which issues are meant to be plain. Independents refused to sign the Westminster Confession of Faith because they held to a different form of church government.

It therefore seems that the regulative principle in its historical form goes beyond what Scripture requires. It is quite possible to apply scriptural principles to any action, tradition or theory not specifically mentioned in the New Testament, and by that means recognize the full authority of Scripture over church worship and government. Any practice that accords with these principles does not violate Scripture. The church can thus remain faithful yet able to be the church for every generation and culture. Furthermore, this conclusion allows us to accept fellow believers who worship differently from us as not necessarily displeasing God.

denominations

We now turn to the most visible form of our diversity, the plethora of Christian denominations. The rise of denominations has occasionally been necessary in the history of the church, but usually they result from the human weakness and sinfulness of Christians. Sometimes we disagree out of error or weakness. Sometimes we are argumentative, we refuse to give way when we should, and we find it easier to start a new grouping than to work out the problem within the structures of the old. Denominations are often the result of reading the Word of God in and through a specific cultural or historical situation.

The founding of a new denomination is frequently prompted by social as well as theological pressures. New religious movements, whether they be the independent churches of West Africa in the twentieth century or Brownists in England in the seventeenth, usually arise among the poor. The Anabaptists broke with Luther for political as well as theological reasons. Furthermore, the factors that lead people to join one denomination rather than another are often social. H. Richard Niebuhr, in *The Social Sources of Denominationalism*, demonstrates that as the denominations spread across North America, their membership was strongly class-oriented.

These socially and historically conditioned interpretations can be petrified in a comprehensive statement of faith, or a body of tradition, hallowed by the names of the great ones who began the denomination. In the 1980s, Roman Catholic theologian Hans Küng began to put forward such a theory to explain our present situation. In science, as a new paradigm develops, so the previous one dies. This has not happened in the church. Instead, the patristic Greek paradigm is still with us, embodied in the Orthodox churches; the medieval paradigm in the traditional Catholic church; the Reformation paradigm in the traditional Protestant and evangelical churches; and the Enlightenment paradigm in liberal theology.[31]

Going further than Küng, we can apply this idea to the smaller units too. For instance, the Scottish Presbyterian Church has preserved the theological work of Calvin in Geneva in the sixteenth century, echoed in the seventeenth-century Westminster Confession of Faith and the Longer and Shorter Catechisms as the church's 'subordinate standards'. Along with these doctrinal statements are traditions such as the frequency of and rules surrounding the administration of communion. The Anglican churches have done similar things in their use of the Thirty-nine Articles and the

Prayer Book. In fact, each denomination today reflects to a greater or lesser degree a historical and cultural interpretation of the Scriptures preserved by its documents and traditions.

the case against denominations

Although a few writers have sought to defend denominations as the best way to be the church today, most believe that the case against them is strong.

First, they seem to contradict the intention of God. It is hard to read the New Testament without seeing that one church was built on the foundation of the one Christ and that we are commanded to maintain that unity. There was a specific attempt to create two parties in the church on the basis of a secondary issue when Peter came to Antioch and, as a Jew, refused to eat with the Gentile Christians. This would have meant two breakings of bread in one city, two congregations, and Paul rightly withstood him to his face.

The question then presents itself: should individuals and congregations subject themselves to the authority of institutions not sanctioned by God and outside his original intention for the church? Those who do not apply the regulative principle could doubtless make out a case if, on balance, denominations are beneficial to the church and not detrimental to it, but this is a difficult argument to maintain.

Secondly, denominations damage concepts of church membership and church discipline. There is so much choice. When there was only one church in a city, membership and commitment to one another meant a great deal. Discipline or removal from the fellowship was awful to contemplate. Nowadays, membership, mutual accountability and pastoral authority mean little. Church discipline is rarely exercised because a dissatisfied Christian can go down the street to another church and start again. While denominations require loyalty to themselves, their very existence undermines a more important loyalty to the local church or congregation.

Thirdly, denominations limit the extent of our fellowship and interaction with other Christians. We worship only with those who belong to our group. Loyalty to denomination-wide organizations is also encouraged, so that a Baptist woman meets mostly Baptist women, and a Presbyterian young person meets mostly Presbyterian young people. Our experience of God is therefore ghettoized except for occasional united services or interdenominational events. Such services, however, give us either too much or too little. If we do not feel free to worship together, once or twice a year is too much. If we do, once or twice a year is nowhere near enough.

As we have already seen, this segregation of Christians who are different cuts everyone off from what would otherwise be a deeper understanding of the love of God. Our individual experiences, arising out of our differences, when shared with each other lead us into deeper spiritual understanding.

Fourthly, denominations damage our service and witness to the world. The duplication of activities and resources within one town can be immense: too many church buildings less than half full; too many Christian youth groups struggling to keep youngsters in their church; too much evangelism done by lone congregations to keep their numbers up.

More importantly, the very existence of our disunity damages our presentation of the gospel. It seems incompatible with the gospel of reconciliation and Christian fellowship that the church preaches. The fact that Christians cannot agree, worship or work together is a poor witness to the reconciling power of the cross. When animosity and a sectarian attitude are also present, the damage is great.

all together in one place

Perhaps the simplest and most profound way of expressing New Testament unity is that all Christians in any one place should worship together in full fellowship, and that they should be in fellowship with all other true churches across the world, accepting and being accepted by them.

This double formula owes its origin to a lecture by Lesslie Newbigin in 1954. Under the heading 'The proper form of church unity' he writes: 'First … it must be such that all who are in Christ in any place are, in that place, visibly one fellowship; and secondly … it must be such that each local community is so ordered and so related to the whole that its fellowship with all Christ's people everywhere, and with all who have gone before and will come after, is made clear.'[32]

The formula exercised a significant influence within the World Council of Churches until the 1960s. After Vatican 2, the increasing role of the Roman Catholic Church in the ecumenical movement shifted attention away from the local expression of unity towards interconfessional dialogue, for instance between Lutherans and Anglicans, Pentecostals and Catholics.

Our 'local churches' today are not the natural heirs of the New Testament local church. They are gatherings of those Christians in one locality who are able to sign the papers of membership. These (with a few exceptions) are rules and statements of faith designed to exclude from membership other local Christians who disagree with them on a number of secondary issues. In this respect, they are more akin to clubs than to biblical local churches.

As we have seen, there is evidence that even in New Testament times there were a number of congregations in any one large city. The church in Rome, for instance, seemed to consist of various 'churches' in different houses (Rom. 16:5), all under the pastoral oversight of the elders of the church in Rome. Can we move back towards this model? After all, which is more important: fellowship with local believers who are one with us in Christ and the fundamentals of the faith, or fellowship with far-flung believers who are also one with us on secondary distinctives? Until this is accepted as an ideal by all and we begin to work it out in each locality, we shall have to live with the present messy situation rather than with what God intended. The practical difficulties involved in this aim are immense, but they must be the second consideration, not the first. The body of believers that sees such an aim as God's will will then have sufficient motivation to tackle the many problems to be faced.

The existence of denominations forces us to face two difficult situations.

staying in or coming out

First, there is the issue of evangelicals within mixed denominations. Usually, the differences between denominations are of a secondary order, but differences within denominations are often of a fundamental nature. For instance, Baptists and Anglicans differ over church government, sacramental matters such as the administration of baptism, and the relationship of the church to the state. Within each of these groupings, however, there are both evangelicals and those who deny the divinity of Christ and his atonement.

Some accept the reality of this situation and are content to serve the church through their denomination. Some would regard it as unwise for evangelicals to remain in such a situation. Others would go further and argue that evangelicals who stay in are guilty by association with those who deny a fundamental truth. A few would go even further and separate themselves from those who do not separate from denominations which contain error. This is the 'second-degree separation' espoused by Peter Masters and others.[33]

The situation is complicated, and there are sincere Christians in each of these four positions. But the Scriptures appeal for no judging of other believers if they are honestly trying to please God in a complicated situation (Rom. 14:1–13). This issue itself should be regarded as a secondary matter, not big enough to cause us to break fellowship with those who cannot agree with us about the way forward.

evangelicals and Roman Catholics

Secondly, how do we respond when faced with a denomination whose official position is seen to oppose evangelical fundamentals? There are over two and half times as many Roman Catholics as all Protestants put together, so this is not an issue we can easily ignore. In the last few years, high-profile conversions to Roman Catholicism have placed the question even higher on the agenda.

At the time of the Reformation a number of attempts were made to reconcile the Roman Catholic Church and the Reformers, but these fell away when the Council of Trent (1545–63) fixed Catholic dogma in an anti-Reformation form. In England during the reign of Elizabeth I a virulent antipathy to the Catholic Church developed for political reasons, helped by the graphic accounts in Foxe's martyrology. In Ireland, this hostility between Catholic and Protestant became even more marked by virtue of the fact that each religeous view existed almost exclusively within opposing social communities. Historical factors such as these often heighten the feeling with which evangelicals react to Roman Catholicism.

The last twenty years have seen a number of attempts to revisit the issue in a non-partisan way, starting with the 'Evangelical–Roman Catholic Dialogue on Mission' (1977–84), composed of prominent evangelicals and Catholics. It was of the opinion that there was more agreement than had been hitherto supposed, but that it had been hidden by misrepresentation, laziness and a refusal to listen carefully enough. They concluded, however, that there was sufficient disagreement on important gospel issues to preclude evangelism together. Joint action on social issues, Bible translation, the media and in other areas was to be encouraged, along with prayer together in a neutral place for all who belong to Christ.

On 29 March 1994, the result of a two-year consultation entitled 'Evangelicals and Catholics Together: The Christian Mission in the Third Millennium' was published. It had the backing of a number of evangelical leaders, and took an even more eirenic line than the consultation of 1977–84. It too noted major differences of understanding, but affirmed that evangelicals and Catholics in North America are brothers and sisters in Christ and should witness together. This produced a storm of protest from many evangelical quarters.

The Roman Catholic Church is a complex institution, and relationships with it can exist on a number of levels. The ordinary member may or may not be a member of Christ's church, as is true of Protestants also. The Reformers never denied this; indeed, many of them were themselves members of the Catholic Church for some time. The theologians of the church represent a second level, partially at least controlled from the centre, but with much greater freedom of expression than is found in official pronouncements. Evangelicals can relate directly to these as individuals and as academics. Specific groups with an evangelical agenda have recently arisen in the Roman Catholic Church. We have already mentioned charismatic groupings. More recently a group calling itself Evangelical Catholics has formed, comprising Catholics who have signed the comprehensively evangelical Lausanne Covenant. Whatever we believe about whether they should remain in their church or not, we can relate to all these in the same way as to other fellow evangelicals with whom we disagree on non-fundamental matters.

The *magisterium*, or teaching office of the church exercised through councils and the papacy, is the area of greatest difficulty for evangelicals. While Vatican 2 has done much to modify it, the *magisterium* still stands for significant divergences from the evangelical faith on fundamental matters. To the extent that the local congregation in the Catholic system is representative of the Catholic Church at its centre, most evangelicals have had difficulties in relating on a congregation-to-congregation basis, although Calvin in his letter to Cardinal Sadoleto acknowledged the possibility that a local congregation of Roman Catholics could be a true church.[34]

This chapter, and the book, must close with an appeal to the unifying power of the one Christ. Those saved by his death, born again by his Spirit and destined for his heaven will always regard these shared blessings as immeasurably more important than the lesser matters that divide.

conclusions

1. *We must not be complacent about the present situation*. We cannot rest in the idea of a solely invisible unity of all God's people. It is this very invisible unity which demands visible expression. Because we are family, we ought to be together. The will of God is involved, and so however difficult the task, and however often we have been disappointed, we keep on seeking greater unity.

2. *We need to preserve the category of heresy.* If a person, church or organization denies a fundamental of the faith, that is heresy and cannot be tolerated. Fellowship must be withdrawn. We must ensure that we limit the category of heresy to the fundamentals, however, and that we do not use a dispute on a secondary issue to drag in a dispute on a fundamental. For instance, those who disagree with the ordination of women cannot assume that those who do have abandoned the authority of Scripture because they read it another way. Baptists cannot assume that those who believe in infant baptism have abandoned the doctrine of salvation by faith alone.

3. *Christians should never leave any church easily.* 'The Lord esteems the communion of his church so highly', writes Calvin, 'that he counts as a traitor and apostate from Christianity anyone who arrogantly leaves any Christian society, provided it cherishes the true ministry of Word and sacraments.'[35] Just as there is a sin of heresy, so there is a sin of schism, and neither is to be taken lightly. We should not be looking for a greater diversity of churches but for a greater diversity within the churches we have.

4. *We must not confuse the truth with our understanding of it.* As we saw earlier, theology is not the Word of God, but merely a human attempt to describe and apply that Word in a specific situation and for a specific reason. No-one's doctrine of the infallibility of Scripture is infallible. No-one's understanding of the divinity of Christ is divine.

5. *When people express the faith differently from ourselves, we should not conclude that they are not expressing the faith.* Each group of Christians has a way of expressing its experiences of Christ. Regarding conversion, for instance, some talk of the act of faith, some of accepting Christ, some of choosing Christ, some of coming to Christ or to faith, and some about their repentance. We need to listen carefully for the meaning attached to the stock phrases, and not automatically dismiss others who do not express things as we would expect.

6. *We should not be afraid.* Robert Amess, a prominent Baptist minster deeply involved in the evangelical scene in England, observes that 'Evangelicalism today is not marked by mutual trust and affection but rather distrust, recrimination and animosity. Perfect love drives out fear (1 Jn. 4:18), but I have discovered that for many fear is the order of the day. Fear of their constituency and fear of its leaders. Fear of what men might say. Fear of being labelled "compromising" by some and "uncommitted" by others. The more prevailing question seems to be not "What does the Bible say?" but "What will be my position if I seek to implement it?"'[36] It is hard to please God rather than men and women.

7. *We should offer fellowship as widely as the Word of God allows*. Brothers and sisters should live in mutual acceptance and harmony. We should make it our aim to accept one another as Christ has accepted us (Rom. 15:7), making our offer of fellowship as wide as God's. We can enjoy the diversity, and will probably learn more from Christians who are different than from those who are like us.

8. *We should prefer the interdenominational to the denominational*. We do not have to remain quietly in the boxes manufactured by our forebears. There is a wider church out there and God wants us to be blessed by fellowship with all his children. Loyalty to denominational activities is not necessarily loyalty to Christ and his church.

9. *We should prefer the local to the distant*. It is more important to have fellowship with those Christians who are close at hand than with those of the same denomination who live a hundred miles away.

10. *Love*. Walt Whitman wrote:

> Were you looking to be held together by lawyers?
> Or by an agreement on a paper? Or by arms?
> Nay, nor the world, nor any living thing will so cohere.[37]

The cement of the church can only be love.

notes

1. a diverse society

1. See Lesslie Newbigin, *The Gospel in a Pluralist Society* (London: SPCK, 1989), especially pp. 14–17.
2. See Peter L. Berger, *The Heretical Imperative* (London: Collins, 1980), especially pp. 11–16.
3. Peter L. Berger, *Facing up to Modernity* (Harmondsworth: Penguin, 1979), pp. 167–180.
4. Francis L. K. Hsu, *Clan. Caste and Club* (Princeton: Van Nostrand, 1963).
5. Eric Hobsbawn, *Age of Extremes* (London: Abacus, 1955), pp. 257–263.
6. Alvin Toffler, *Future Shock* (London: Pan, 1974), pp. 32–41.
7. Paul Hiebert, *Anthropological Insights for Missionaries* (Grand Rapids: Baker, 1985), p. 30.
8. *Ibid.*, pp. 42–43.
9. James Clavel, *Shogun* (Sevenoaks: Hodder and Stoughton, 1975), pp. 569–570.
10. Newbigin, *The Gospel in a Pluralist Society*, pp. 27–38.
11. Introductions to postmodernism can be found in Philip Sampson, 'The Rise of Postmodernity', in Philip Sampson, Vinay Samuel and Chris Sugden, *Faith and Modernity* (Oxford: Regnum, 1994), pp. 29–57; Nick Mercer, 'Postmodernity and Rationality: The Final Credits or Just a Commercial Break?' in Anthony Billington, Tony Lane and Max Turner (eds.), *Mission and Meaning* (Carlisle: Paternoster, 1995), pp. 319–338; Bryan S. Turner, *Theories of Modernity and Postmodernity* (London: Sage, 1990).
12. Hobsbawn, *Age of Extremes*, pp. 522–534.
13. Michael Polanyi, *Personal Knowledge* (London: Routledge and Kegan Paul, 1958), pp. vii–viii.
14. Thomas S. Kuhn, *The Structure of Scientific Revolutions* (Chicago: University of Chicago Press, 1962).
15. Jacques Derrida, *Speech and Phenomena* (Evanston: Northwestern University Press, 1973), p. 154.
16. An exhaustive treatment of the whole subject is given in Anthony C. Thiselton, *New Horizons in Hermeneutics* (Grand Rapids: Zondervan, 1992).

17. Hans-Georg Gadamer, 'The Universality of the Hermeneutical Problem', in Josef Bleicher, *Contemporary Hermeneutics* (London: Routledge and Kegan Paul, 1980), pp. 128–140. For Gadamer, Habermas and Ricoeur, see also Thiselton, *New Horizons in Hermeneutics*.
18. Jürgen Habermas, 'The Hermeneutic Claim to Universality', in Bleicher, *Contemporary Herememeutics*, pp. 181–209; Steven Seidman, *Contested Knowledge: Social Theory in the Postmodern Era* (Oxford: Blackwell, 1994), pp. 171–193.
19. Paul Ricoeur, 'Existence and Hermeneutics', in Bleicher, *Contemporary Hermeneutics*, pp. 236–256; Mario J. Valtes, *A Ricoeur Reader* (New York: Harvester Wheatsheaf, 1991).
20. Arthur Koestler, *Darkness at Noon* (London: Vintage, 1994), p. 138.
21. John Hick, 'The Non-Absoluteness of Christianity', in John Hick and Paul F. Knitter (eds.), *The Myth of Christian Uniqueness* (London: SCM, 1987), p. 16–34.
22. Alister E. McGrath, *A Life of John Calvin* (Oxford: Blackwell, 1990), pp. 114–120.

2. the basis for Christian choice

1. Quoted in Anton Wessels, *Images of Jesus* (London: SCM, 1990), p. 88.
2. See previous note.
3. Alister E. McGrath. *A Passion for Truth* (Leicester: IVP, 1996), p. 123.
4. Aloys Grillmeier, *Christ in Christian Tradition*, 1 (London: Mowbrays, 1975), pp. 249–273.
5. Dietrich Bonhoeffer, *Life Together* (London: SCM, 1972).
6. Thomas à Kempis, *The Imitation of Christ* (Harmondsworth: Penguin, 1968), p. 83.
7. John Hick and Paul F. Knitter (eds.), *The Myth of Christian Uniqueness* (London: SCM, 1987); Paul F. Knitter, *No Other Name?* (London: SCM, 1985); see also Alan Race, *Christians and Religious Pluralism* (London: SCM, 1983), pp. 70–105.
8. Knitter, *No Other Name?*, pp. 23–36, 91.
9. Lesslie Newbigin, *The Gospel in a Pluralist Society* (London: SPCK, 1989), p. 165.
10. Karl Barth, *Church Dogmatics* I.2 (Edinburgh: T. and T. Clark, 1956), pp. 280–361.
11. Howard Lindsell, 'The Missionary Imperative', in Norman A.

Horner (ed.), *Protestant Concurrents in Mission* (Nashville: Abingdon, 1968), p. 57.

12. Austin Flannery (ed.), *Vatican Council II: The Conciliar and Post-Conciliar Documents* (Dublin: Dominican Publications, 1975), pp. 366–368.
13. Karl Rahner, *Theological Investigations* 5 (London: Darton Longman and Todd, 1966), pp.118–131; 6 (1969), pp. 392–394.
14. Sir Norman Anderson, *Christianity and World Religions* (Leicester: IVP, 1970); Clark H. Pinnock, *A Wideness in God's Mercy* (Grand Rapids: Zondervan, 1992); Peter Cotterell, *Mission and Meaninglessness* (London: SPCK, 1990); Charles H. Kraft, *Christianity in Culture* (New York: Orbis, 1979), pp. 240–245; John Saunders, *No Other Name* (Grand Rapids: Eerdmans, 1992).
15. See I. Howard Marshall (ed.), *New Testament Interpretation* (Exeter: Paternoster, 1977).
16. On these issues see D. A. Carson and John D. Woodbridge (eds.), *Scripture and Truth* (rev. edn Grand Rapids: Baker, 1992); Carl F. H. Henry, *Revelation and the Bible* (London: Tyndale, 1959).
17. Anthony C. Thiselton, 'The New Hermeneutic', in Donald K. McKim, *A Guide to Contemporary Hermeneutics* (Grand Rapids: Eerdmans, 1986), pp. 78–107.
18. Ernst Fuchs, 'The New Testament and the Hermeneutical Problem', in James M. Robinson and J. B. Cobb Jr (eds.), *New Frontiers in Theology* II: *The New Hermeneutic* (New York: Harper and Row, 1964), p. 117.

3. ethics

1. For a discussion of some of these medical ethical problems see M. Dominic Beer (ed.), *Christian Choices in Healthcare* (Leicester: IVP, 1995); John Wilkinson, *Christian Ethics in Health Care* (Edinburgh, Handsel, 1988).
2. Norman L. Geisler, *Christian Ethics* (Leicester: IVP, 1989), especially pp. 17–134.
3. Joseph Fletcher, *Situation Ethics* (London: SCM, 1966), p. 13.
4. *Ibid.*, p. 133.
5. For an analysis of situation ethics, see William Barclay, *Ethics in a Permissive Society* (London: Collins, 1972), pp. 69–91.
6. Josef Blank, 'Unity and Plurality in New Testament Ethics', *Concilium* 150 (October 1981), pp. 65–71.
7. J. B. Harrison, 'Temperance Movements', in John Macquarrie (ed.), *A Dictionary of Christian Ethics* (London: SCM, 1967), pp. 339–341.

8. Alasdair MacIntyre, *After Virtue* (London: Duckworth, 1981), pp. 1–2.
9. Zygmunt Bauman, *Postmodern Ethics* (Oxford: Blackwell, 1993). See also Philip Goodchild, 'Christian Ethics in the Postmodern Condition', *Studies in Christian Ethics* 8.1 (1955), pp. 20–32.
10. '*Kosmos*', in Gerhard Kittel (ed.), *Theological Dictionary of the New Testament* 3 (Grand Rapids: Eerdmans, 1966), pp. 860–898.
11. Paul Hiebert, *Anthropological Insights for Missionaries* (Grand Rapids: Baker, 1985), pp. 190–191.
12. Quoted in J. I. Packer, *Laid-Back Religion?* (Leicester: IVP, 1987), pp. 45–70.
13. Jim Wallis, *The Call to Conversion* (Tring: Lion, 1981), pp. 24–25.
14. Helga Dittmar, *The Social Psychology of Material Possessions: To Have is to Be* (New York: St Martin's Press, 1992), p. 13.
15. A good introduction to Francis is J. R. H. Moorman, *Francis of Assisi* (London: SPCK, 1963). An interesting discussion of Francis from a liberation viewpoint is Leonardo Boff, *Saint Francis* (London: SCM, 1982).

4. theology

1. For a brief survey of different forms of church structure, see Donald Macleod, 'Church Government', in Sinclair B. Ferguson and David F. Wright (eds.) *New Dictionary of Theology* (Leicester: IVP, 1988), pp. 143–146.
2. Eugene Nida, *Customs, Culture and Christianity* (London: Tyndale, 1954); Charles H. Kraft, *Christianity in Culture* (New York: Orbis, 1979).
3. Charles H. Kraft, 'Dynamic Equivalent Churches', in C. H. Kraft and T. N. Wisley (eds.), *Readings in Dynamic Indigeneity* (Pasadena: William Carey Library, 1979), pp. 87–111.
4. Kosuke Koyama, *Three Mile an Hour God* (London: SCM, 1979), p. 7.
5. James D. G. Dunn, *Unity and Diversity in the New Testament* (London: SCM, 1977); D. A. Carson, 'Unity and Diversity in the New Testament', in D. A. Carson and J. D. Woodbridge (eds.), *Scripture and Truth* (rev. edn Grand Rapids: Baker, 1992), pp. 65–100.
6. Graham Cheesman, 'Dynamic Christology', *Themelios* 8.1 (September 1982), pp. 10–15.
7. David Tracy, 'Some Concluding Reflections', in Hans Küng and David Tracy, *Paradigm Change in Theology* (Edinburgh: T. and T. Clark, 1989), pp. 461–462.
8. Quoted in G. Facre, *Ecumenical Faith in Evangelical Perspective* (Grand

Rapids: Eerdmans, 1993), p. 210.

9. David Tracy, *Blessed Rage for Order* (New York: Seabury, 1975); *The Analogical Imagination* (London: SCM, 1981).
10. Gustavo Gutiérrez, *A Theology of Liberation* (London: SCM, 1988), p. xiii.
11. Juan Luís Segundo, 'The Hermeneutic Circle', in Dean William Fern (ed.), *Third World Liberation Theologies* (New York: Orbis, 1986), pp. 64–92.
12. Frantz Fanon, *The Wretched of the Earth* (Harmondsworth: Penguin, 1965), p. 74.
13. For a critical dialogue with these ideas from an evangelical perspective, see J. Andrew Kirk, *Liberation Theology* (Basingstoke: Marshall, Morgan and Scott, 1985).
14. S. B. Bevans, *Models of Contextual Theology* (New York: Orbis, 1992).
15. *Ibid.* See also R. J. Schreiter, *Constructing Local Theologies* (London: SCM, 1985).

5. mission

1. David J. Bosch, *Transforming Mission* (New York: Orbis, 1991), pp. 368–507, offers a comprehensive analysis of the present situation in missiology.
2. Quoted in *ibid.*, p. 404.
3. Quoted in *ibid.*, p. 405.
4. See especially *Evangelism and Social Responsibility* (World Evangelical Fellowship and Lausanne Committee for World Evangelization, 1982), report of the International Consultation on the Relationship between Evangelism and Social Responsibility held in Grand Rapids in June 1982.
5. Tom Stransky, 'Missio Dei', in Nicholas Lossky *et al.* (eds.), *Dictionary of the Ecumenical Movement* (Geneva: WCC Publications, 1991), pp. 687–689.
6. Donald McGavran, *Understanding Church Growth* (Grand Rapids: Eerdmans, 2nd edn 1980).
7. David J. Hesselgrave, *Today's Choices for Tomorrow's Mission* (Grand Rapids: Zondervan, 1988), p. 135.
8. The best one-volume study of mission theology is Stephen Neill, *A History of Christian Missions* (Harmondsworth: Penguin, 1964).
9. J. I. Packer, *Laid-Back Religion?* (Leicester: IVP, 1987), pp. 71–90. See also Garry Friesen, *Decision Making and the Will of God* (Portland: Multnomah, 1980).

10. Quoted in G. S. M. Walker, *The Growing Storm* (London: Paternoster, 1961), p. 223.
11. John Stott, *Christian Mission in the Modern World* (London: Falcon, 1975), pp. 58–69; J. Verkuyl, *Contemporary Missiology* (Grand Rapids: Eerdmans, 1978), pp. 362–368.
12. John Cyril Sladden, *Boniface of Devon* (Exeter: Paternoster, 1980).
13. E. H. Carr, *What is History?* (Harmondsworth: Penguin, 1961). See also David Bebbington, *Patterns in History* (2nd edn Leicester: Apollos, 1990).
14. See D. A. Carson, *The Gagging of God* (Leicester: IVP, 1996).
15. David Bebbington, 'Evangelical Christianity and the Enlightenment', in Martin Eden and David F. Wells (eds.), *The Gospel in the Modern World* (Leicester: IVP, 1991), pp. 66–78; Dave Tomlinson, *The Post-Evangelical* (London: SPCK, 1995); Alister E. McGrath, *A Passion for Truth* (Leicester: Apollos, 1996).
16. Charles Hodge, *Systematic Theology* (London: Nelson, 1873), p. 1.
17. D. A. Carson, *The Gagging of God*, p. 96.
18. Roger Lundin, 'The Pragmatics of Postmodernity', in Timothy R. Phillips and Dennis L. Okholm (eds.), *Christian Apologetics in the Postmodern World* (Downers Grove: IVP, 1995), p. 15.
19. Paul G. Hiebert, *Anthropological Insights for Missionaries* (Grand Rapids: Baker, 1985), p. 54.
20. Donald McGavran, *Understanding Church Growth* (Grand Rapids: Eerdmans, 2nd edn 1980), p. 223.
21. C. René Padilla, 'The Unity of the Church and the Homogeneous Unit Principle', in Wilbert R. Shenk (ed.), *Exploring Church Growth* (Grand Rapids: Eerdmans, 1983), pp. 285–303.
22. Lesslie Newbigin, *The Gospel in a Pluralist Society* (London: SPCK, 1989), pp. 222–233.
23. Quoted in Philip D. Kenneson, 'There's No Such Thing as Objective Truth and it's a Good Thing Too', in Phillips and Okholm, *Christian Apologetics in the Postmodern World*, p. 169, my emphasis.
24. David F. Wells, *No Place for Truth* (Grand Rapids: Eerdmans; Leicester: IVP, 1993); Mark Noll, *The Scandal of the Evangelical Mind* (Grand Rapids: Eerdmans, 1994); McGrath, *A Passion for Truth*.
25. Tertullian, *Apology* XXXVII, in *The Ante-Nicene Fathers* 3 (Edinburgh: T. and T. Clark, 1989), p. 45.

6. unity

1. David Barrett, *World Christian Encylopedia* (Oxford: Oxford

University Press, 1982), pp. 15–17. Barrett updates his statistics once a year in the *International Bulletin of Missionary Research*.

2. Huldrych Zwingli, *On the Clarity and Certainty of the Word of God*. See also Alister E. McGrath, *Reformation Thought: An Introduction* (Oxford: Blackwell, 1993), pp. 151–155.
3. Quoted in Tom Stransky, 'World Council of Churches', in Nicholas Lossky (ed.), *Dictionary of the Ecumenical Movement* (Geneva: WCC Publications, 1991), pp. 1083–1090.
4. *Ibid.*
5. Austin Flannery, *Vatican Council II: The Conciliar and Post-Conciliar Documents* (Dublin: Dominican Publications, 1987), pp. 359, 455–456.
6. Quoted in *The Christian*, 19 October 1962.
7. See J. R. W. Stott, *Explaining the Lausanne Covenant* (London: Scripture Union, 1975).
8. Iain H. Murray, *D. Martyn Lloyd-Jones: The Fight of Faith, 1939–1981* (Edinburgh: Banner of Truth, 1990), pp. 523–528.
9. See David Bebbington, *Evangelicalism in Modern Britain* (London: Unwin Hyman, 1989), pp. 249–251.
10. *Ibid.*, p. 247.
11. Michael Harper, *That We May Be One* (London: Hodder and Stoughton, 1983).
12. Published, respectively, by Kingsway (Eastbourne), Baker (Grand Rapids) and Bridgepoint (Wheaton).
13. Gilbert W. Kirby, *All One in Christ?* (Eastbourne: Kingsway, 1984), p. 124.
14. H. Richard Niebuhr, *The Social Sources of Denominationalism* (New York: Meridian, 1957), p. 15.
15. Quoted in Amess, *One in the Truth*, p. 149.
16. Calvin, *Institutes* IV.i.12, trans. F. L. Battles, ed. J. T. McNeill (London: SCM, 1961), 2, p. 1026.
17. Quoted in Yves Congar, *Diversity and Communion* (London: SCM, 1984), pp. 111–112.
18. The Thirty-nine Articles, VI and XX.
19. Quoted in Congar, *Diversity and Communion,* p. 118.
20. Flannery (ed.), *Vatican Councill II*, p. 462.
21. C. H. Spurgeon, *Speeches* (London: Passmore and Alabaster, 1878), p. 14.
22. Leonard Verduin, *The Reformers and their Stepchildren* (Exeter: Paternoster, 1964), p. 217.

23. Richard Baxter, dedication to the Bishop of Winchester of *The True Way of Concord of all the Christian Churches* (1697), quoted in Congar, *Diversity and Communion*, p. 109.
24. Quoted in Congar, *Diversity and Communion*, p. 99.
25. Quoted in *ibid.*, p. 76. See also Eric Hobsbawn, *Age of Extremes* (London: Abacus, 1995), p. 539.
26. Jürgen Moltmann, 'Theological Proposals Towards the Resolution of the *Filioque* Controversy', in Lukas Vischer (ed.), *Spirit of God, Spirit of Christ* (London: SPCK, 1981), pp. 164–173.
27. Donald G. Bloesch, *Essentials of Evanglical Theology* (New York: Harper and Row, 1978), 1, p. 9; Robert Webber, *Evangelicals on the Canterbury Trail* (Texas: Word, 1985).
28. Flannery (ed.), *Vatican Council II*, p. 755.
29. Quoted in Michael Sansom, *Why Liturgical Worship Anyway?* (Bramcote: Grove, 1984).
30. Iain Murray, 'Scripture and Things Indifferent', in *Diversity in Unity*, papers read at the Puritan and Reformed Studies Conference, December 1963, p. 16.
31. Hans Küng, 'What Does a Change of Paradigm Mean?' in Hans Küng and David Tracy (eds.), *Paradigm Change in Theology* (Edinburgh: T. and T. Clark, 1989), pp. 121–219.
32. Lesslie Newbigin, 'All Together in One Place', *Journal of Religion* (January 1955), p. 31.
33. For a fuller discussion of these issues, see Alan F. Gibson (ed.), *The Church and its Unity* (Leicester: IVP, 1992) and Amess, *One in the Truth*, pp. 65–86.
34. J. K. S. Reid (ed.), *Calvin: Theological Treatises* (London: SCM, 1954), p. 241. See also John Armstrong (ed.), *Roman Catholicism* (Chicago: Moody, 1994).
35. Calvin, *Institutes* IV.i.10 (2, p. 145).
36. Amess, *One in the Truth*, p. 11.
37. Walt Whitman, *The Complete Poems* (Harmondsworth: Penguin, 1986), p. 341.

Sowing Reaping Keeping

LAURENCE SINGLEHURST

The Christian gospel is the best news ever told. Yet many of those who hear it perceive it as a threat. Laurence Singlehurst believes that much of the threat would be removed if Christians would respect and understand the people they are approaching.

This short, crisp and often humorous book is full of seeds of wisdom for those who long to help to make permanent disciples for Jesus.

'Pastors and elders will love what this important book does for their church.'
Floyd McClung

'Laurence Singlehurst rightly emphasises the twin importance of strategic thinking and informed prayer. Here is a book that moves beyond the theory of evangelism to its practice.'
from the foreword by Ian Coffey

128 pages *Pocketbook*

Crossway Books

Why Bother With Mission

STEPHEN GAUKROGER

It's not really a good idea to read this book. What chance do you as an ordinary Christian have to make a difference in a needy world? Besides there are a lot more exciting things to be involved in when it comes to your local church.

Surely it's a lot of bother for you to link up with God's world-wide search-and-rescue mission – whether in a supportive, informed role, or as a mission worker sent out to cross barriers of society, language or geography?

If you can't face an informative, inspiring, heartfelt guide to mission today, and what you can do – avoid this book at all costs, especially if you are an ordinary unheroic Christian (at the moment)!

'A great introduction to understanding and becoming involved in mission.' *Tony Campolo*

'An exciting new book, guaranteed to persuade anyone to become a partner in mission.'
Steve Chalke

Stephen Gaukroger is senior minister of a large Baptist church in Buckinghamshire, England, and formerly President of the Baptist Union of Great Britain. He and his wife Janet have three children.

160 pages *'B' format*

Inter-Varsity Press